LET
THE BOY
SING

LET
THE BOY
SING

Elvis is My Daddy

John Dennis Smith
with Rich Carlburg

TATE PUBLISHING
AND ENTERPRISES, LLC

Published by Tate Publishing & Enterprises, LLC
127 E. Trade Center Terrace | Mustang, Oklahoma 73064 USA
1.888.361.9473 | www.tatepublishing.com

Tate Publishing is committed to excellence in the publishing industry. The company reflects the philosophy established by the founders, based on Psalm 68:11,
"The Lord gave the word and great was the company of those who published it."

Book design copyright © 2013 by Tate Publishing, LLC. All rights reserved.
Cover design by Rodrigo Adolfo
Interior design by Mary Jean Archival

Published in the United States of America

ISBN: 978-1-62563-578-5
1. Biography & Autobiography / General
2. Biography & Autobiography/ Personal Memoirs
13.03.28

Contents

Let the Boy Sing

As I come off stage to greet my fans and have a little conversation in another club/coffeehouse/bar, it happens again, just like every time. "You are such an amazing singer. You remind me of someone. By your accent, you must be from Texas, right?" Another new fan that feels a connection to me. I don't know how it came to be, but with no intent to brag, I have yet to find the room that I cannot own, if I choose to connect with the audience.

"Why, yes, I am from Texas. Nice to meet you. My name is John, John Smith. No, really, John Smith. Do you want to see my driver's license? It says John Smith also."

Sometimes some of the drunk ones still think I am pulling their leg. I'm not. The new fan smiles at the irony and the joke. I smile too. It happens all the time. I'm smiling a different smile. The smile of knowing. They get the joke. I know the whole story. Well, at least most of it. I know that the John came from my dad. He liked the name because it was a strong and biblical name. The Smith, that came from my adopted dad and his wife. That is still only part of the story. "The rest of the story" would tax the mighty resiliency and resources of the likes of Paul Harvey.

How did I end up with the name that is already on the numerous credit card offers I receive in the mail every week? It's not the name on my original birth certificate, but my new birth certificate has John Smith on it. Again, more of the rest of the story. The question runs through my mind for the three thousandth time: "Do I blow your mind and watch your jaw drop with a portion of the story?" Tonight is just pleasant conversation, and before long, we find that we have lived in the same place or know the same people. Again, it almost always happens. I can walk into a room and be connected to someone. It never takes all six of the degrees of separation. I only need two or three at the most.

The smile of knowing, the one that I mentioned. That is another thing that I share. This I only share with a few, and the funny thing is that they had the smile before I did. My longtime manager showed up when I was still a child and made a deal with the man that gave me the "Smith." He smiled a nice smile, and I liked him. I did not know what his smile really meant. It is the same smile that I now have. I knew that he came to see John Smith. I did not know that the man that named me John was the one that sent him. He shook my father's hand. He was to watch and watch out for me. The man that named me Smith, he knows too. He gave me his name, but his nephew gave me life and the rest of my name. My birth mom knows more than anyone, but I wouldn't even know that she is my mom or see that kind of smile for twenty more years. Her smile would be attached to part of the story that I don't even know yet—the part of the story about who my father was. Comments, jokes, and comparisons have been made all my life, and that is all that I think that they are. My backup singers. They knew. They smile. They are sent to watch me too. They sang backup for my father. Everybody smiles. Very few tell the tale. My photographer smiles, and he is on the other side of the camera. He smiles because he knows both of the people that brought me to life, and he sees them in me. I smile my smile of knowing, but sometimes I wish that more people had stopped grinning and had started talking. I would have liked to have known more of my story so I could have known more about the players in my life before they were gone. They are amazing people with their own stories. Stories that have already filled books. I would like to have heard more from them and not have to be constantly assembling the pieces, bit by bit, over the years.

Now it is my time, and the stories between the lines in many other books are coming to life with the telling of my story. My story is not to take away from anyone else. It is to add to the story that already is. To fill in the blanks. To answer questions. To finish what was started so many years ago, in a small town, on a dark night. When two people held on to each other to find something real, in a time of madness, in their lives. That is where I got my start, and ironically, I spent years trying to find the same thing for myself. My story begins long before I found out that a family friend that I occasionally saw was really my mom. When I finally met her as my mom, I learned part of the mystery. That I have a famous father. Then I found out that my father is Elvis Presley. I am still surprised that I didn't have more of an emotional reaction to this news. There are lots of interesting family stories in the South. I was busy with my own life and success, and it struck me at the moment as one more story. Well, that makes sense. I get compared to him enough when I sing. This is interesting. I remember not giving it too much thought. After all, I was planning on becoming a bigger star than him anyway. Regardless of my initial reaction, it took several years for the impact of this news to weave its way through my life.

I have gone through my life with a lot of questions, and even more cryptic answers or half answers, that leave me with even more questions about me. I am not trying to find out who really shot President Kennedy or find the Holy Grail. I just want to know about me. Me and my life. It doesn't seem too difficult to me.

Only recently I asked my mom for proof of where I came from. She told me that I have had the proof all along.

"I don't mean my talent or the similarities to the dad I didn't really know. I mean proof. Something I can show to people. Something that can't be written off as an interesting coincidence." Again, she tells me that I have the proof in my possession.

"What?"

"You know that saying in the frame? The one about what it means to be a mom? Why do you think you have that and I, your mom, don't? There's your proof."

"Mom, it talks about being a mother. How is that proof?"

"Not what it says. What it says on the back."

"There's nothing on the back. There's a hole to hang it on the wall. Come on, Mom. Stop messing around."

"Take it out of the frame, son. It is written on the back."

I take it carefully out of the frame and turn it over. There, in faded pencil, written in the hand of our old maid, is a note from my grandmother to my mom. It is hard to read and made even harder by my shaking hands. It tells my mom what it means to be a mother and how my grandmother knows what my mom is experiencing. Then it mentions me, and she writes that if there is ever any question about where that boy comes from, "you just tell them to let that boy sing."

I call my good friend Rich and tell him that he is not going to believe this. He better get over here right now.

"Thanks, Mom."

Now this may never hold up in court or the court of public opinion, but if you are like me, you have a mom. If your mom is like my mom, you don't ever question her intent. A mother is to care for her children. During the times since we have been reunited, we have big doses of it. Like she is still trying to make up for the years we missed. It is said that a mother always knows about her children. Well, this child knows his mom and knows the character of this woman. I know what this story means to her and to me. If you want to question the motives of the woman that gave me life, I invite you to get after it and go right ahead…right after you get done questioning the character and motives of your own mom.

"Thanks, Mom."

My life has been full of people caring for me and caring about me. I have my longtime music manager, HT, who made a promise to my father and my father's uncle, who was my adopted dad. He would watch and watch out for me. He has had to walk the line of keeping his promise and his father-like loyalty to me. He promised not to say anything, but that has not kept him from dropping hints and sending me personal items from Elvis and his family that have great sentimental value. The kind of things that would be passed on from a father to a son. I may have missed out on my paternal father, but thanks to him, I have many items that are from the family. This is not the only references to where I came from. There are Ray Walker and Sherrill Nielsen, names that are not the most famous, but if you know much about Elvis, these are people that are intimately connected to the King. These people have been there all along and have dropped hints along the way. There is also no other reasonable explanation for their ongoing relationship with me.

Welcome to my story. If you have one-tenth of the fun reading it that I have had living it, you are in for quite a ride. This is my story. The cover says a lot, and I want to be clear. I am not the first to make this claim. I know that. The world knows that. I am not here to trade on my father's name or take anything away from him. I am here to add to what was begun many years ago. There is no bad guy in this story. There are people trying to survive and carve out a life for themselves. I am here to give my father something that he did not see. I am here to carry on and to give him a legacy of a son that is continuing what was started. A son that appreciates all that he is given and is grateful for the chance to show the world what is possible when you hold on to your dreams and have the love and support of those around you, especially the ones that cared for Elvis in his life. Those that know the man and the truth and did not judge the image.

Welcome to my story. You have been invited to take a look into my life and hear some amazing stories. This book has been a long time coming for many reasons. It has not been an easy story to tell. Not for the obvious reasons, but for a deeply personal reason. In the telling of my story, I have to open up about myself. I have learned to keep my guard up, to protect myself. Not many people get to see the me that is not the performer. I am naturally shy about myself. I enjoy what others have to say about me, but I am reluctant to talk about my own talent. For years I disregarded the praise of others and told myself they were just being nice. I have finally been convinced that for this story to be told, I have to let my guard down and reveal some private moments and feelings. Along this journey, I have also come to believe in my own gifts as well as the talent I have received. One would think that this would be the easiest thing to realize. I remember as recently as four years ago having this conversation with Rich. We were in his garage while he was building our first guitar. He was telling me that I needed to start believing in myself more and to start associating with people that were more like me. I had a tendency to surround myself with people that did not expect too much from me. Rich was telling me that in order for me to step into the destiny that is meant for me and to reach my God-given potential, I needed to start believing in me and to start demanding more from myself. I told him that I was not sure if I believed that about myself. He seemed genuinely surprised that I did not have the same belief in myself that the rest of the people around us did. Before you start to question my lack of belief in my own talent, look at all of the people in the entertainment business that suffer from self-esteem issues or don't believe that anyone loves them. When I heard about the demise and death of Whitney Houston,

I sent a message to Rich, asking him to make sure that the same thing never happens to me. I could identify with her struggle for love and acceptance. The ability to let people love you as a person and not just the performer. It has taken all this time for me to finally believe what others have told me for years. I am learning that you will only go as far as your own belief will take you.

This book is about me as an adopted boy growing up and, in the process, learning I am the son of Elvis Presley. I find out that I have inherited some of the same charm and musical ability as my father. My story explores the parallels in his and my lives, the people in common, and the numerous coincidences that follow the steps of my life. My life is a part of the legacy that Elvis left behind. It will also explain why this story is just now being told.

My longtime producer and manager William Harrison Tyner (HT) has been a key player in my story. HT started his career in music as part of a group called the Landsman in California. Elvis was on the rise and had heard about HT and wanted to hire him. HT's response was that if Elvis wanted him, he better ask HT himself. One day, HT was taken to the Burbank airport and taken out onto the tarmac, where he walked up the stairs to a waiting plane. When he reached the top of the stairs, Elvis stepped out of the plane, shook HT's hand, and said that he was told that HT needed a personal request from him to come work for him. This was that personal request, and was that good enough for HT. HT indicated that this request was just fine, and they shook hands, and HT walked back down the stairs. He stayed with Elvis in various capacities all the way until the end, and to this day, he still carries on with people that were close to the King. As you will see, HT is a central part of many of the stories of my life. The same handshake that Elvis shared with HT was used when HT shook hands with my adopted dad years later, with a promise that HT made to Elvis in between these two handshakes. Here are a couple of the stories that HT was a part of.

One day in Nashville, HT and I were sitting in a restaurant discussing the events of the upcoming day. Later in the day, I was to perform a show. I told HT that my mom was coming. HT said, "John, Etta [my adopted mom, Etta Smith] passed years ago. You know that."

"No. My mom!" was my reply.

HT did not respond and sat quietly for a few minutes until Zona Marie walked in. To my knowledge, nobody had any idea who my birth mom was. Zona walks in, and HT gets up, meets her across the floor, gives her a big hug, and says, "Zona, how many years has it been?" This left me to wonder, *What else is there about my life that I don't know yet?*

On another occasion, HT and I are at Mitch's house. Mitch Kyrum was my photographer. He also was a personal photographer to Elvis. I am looking through an album of pictures that Mitch has taken. I spy a picture of my mom. "Hey, that's my mom! What are you doing with a picture of my mom!?"

"Come on, John, there are lots of pretty girls in Vegas. How could that be your mom?" was HT's answer.

"That's my mom. I know her! That's her! I have seen that coat she is wearing! That's her!"

At this point, Mitch looks across at HT and says, "You know, H, one of these days you are going to have to tell this boy a story."

At this point in my life, Zona Marie had already told me that Elvis was my daddy. What I was just now finding out was that the two of us were not the only ones that knew. I seemed to be surrounded by others that also had Elvis in common with me. You start looking at people differently and wondering what secret is going to stroll around the corner next. It is eerie at times knowing that the people around you may know more about your life than you do. And why? What was the coercion to stay in my life, all the while keeping the deepest secrets so carefully? Even to this day, these secrets are still kept.

In 2010, an event occurred that shows how deeply held these secrets are. A gentleman working with me met with HT and Ray Walker. Late one night, after I had left to go to bed, this gentleman leaned forward and said, "I think we all know why we are here. Is Elvis really his daddy?" At this question, the room grew still. HT looked down at the table. Ray Walker got up and, without a word, and left the room. Finally, HT looked up and informed the gentleman that we do not discuss this topic here. I learned about the details of this conversation while HT was chewing my ass out the next morning.

Ray Walker signs a picture to me. It says "You are one of a kind, the kind we are." No one close to me will deny my paternity. However, if you are one of the keepers of the secrets, you are not at liberty to confirm it. The keepers do one thing though. They have been instrumental in seeing that the boy is allowed to sing. And sing I do. One of many descriptions of my performing is this: "He will wrap you up in his voice and take you to a place where music is as it should be."

After performing "An American Trilogy" one night, the review the next day was that there have only been two baritones that can hit the high C note in this song. One of them is Elvis Presley, and the other was seen last night, in the person of John Dennis Smith. But that is another of many coincidences that my friends who know me best call "just another day in the life of Johnny." It happens over and over, but does not ever become ordinary.

My story starts in Louisiana in 1960, when Elvis meets my mom. I have to rely on the media and personal accounts to know about what was happening. My life had not yet begun, but the events had already been set in motion that would lead to start of a new life. Eisenhower and Nixon were in the White House. Kennedy was elected. And Elvis was the King. Elvis had met my mom at one of his concerts through family friends. On July 3, 1961, I was born to a young nursing student in Edinburg, Texas, in Hidalgo County. My father was there for my birth. This is not an out-of-the-ordinary occurrence. The difference is that this was my birth, and I was the first child born to Elvis Presley. He had his good friend Sherrill Nielsen with him. This was one of the few times that Elvis was not where he was expected to be or scheduled to be.

At sixteen months old, along with my maternal sisters, I was adopted by my paternal uncle and aunt, ID and Etta Smith. ID was the half brother of Gladys, who was Mrs. Vernon Presley.

As is often the case, at the time we are experiencing our lives, we seldom appreciate it for what it is. I loved my life growing up, and I probably didn't make the most of every experience, and I was also a kid. I didn't know what kind of importance to place on events in my life. I just enjoyed each one and looked forward to the next one. It was life, and I was living it. I knew by people's reaction to me that something special was happening around me, but it was all that I had ever known, so I had no concept of the magnitude of what was unfolding around me. I completely expect to be great at what I do. It is not a boastful statement. I know what I can do, and the response of others confirms it. I don't take it for granted, but I do have expectations of myself when it comes time to turn it on. I know that I can deliver. I demand it of myself. I have a God-given talent and gift, and I expect to use it, and anything given by God is not second-rate. Because of that, I have learned to have confidence in my gift.

The stories of my life are many and span a wide variety of people and circumstances. There are so many that it is hard to catalog them. There are many surrounding Elvis and interactions with key people in the life of the King. I know that this is what the public is interested in, and we will get to that. There are also many encounters and friendships that have a life of their own and are amazing in their own right, such as the following:

- Encounters with Hall of Fame football quarterback, Terry Bradshaw
- Going to Juilliard
- Meeting Lawrence Welk
- Developing friendships with the Gatlins
- Writing songs with the Gatlins
- Being told by a successful songwriter, David Briggs, that we were too young and needed to go to Texas and grow up
- Going outside and keying the car that David Briggs was driving to show him how grown up we were…and being sent to Texas to grow up
- Meeting Kenny Rogers

- Being part of the Mandrell Sisters band
- Leaving a band in Texas and having Ty Herndon replace me, but still using my vocals to book the gigs they were playing
- Playing at a Dallas Cowboys charity banquet
- Developing a friendship with Dennis Weaver
- Founding ecolonomics with Dennis Weaver
- Making friends with John Denver
- Playing and working with John Denver
- Befriending the inventor of Craftsman Tools
- Making friends with the owner of JB Weld and her investing in my singing career

These are just some of my stories. Some of these happened under the watchful eyes of those around me, in keeping the promise they made to my dad. A great many of these happened on my own. My friends joke that they can't take me anywhere, that I don't know someone, or that I at least have a friend in common with.

I imagine that people are interested in my life mainly because of my Elvis connection. This is understandable. I am still intrigued by him and all that he accomplished. I would love to sit down with him and find out what he was thinking. I would love to know the whys of what he did and how he lived. Not the stories about him, but what he was thinking. What he thought about me. Why he took care of me and my mom. How he kept an eye on me. If he ever heard me sing. These are questions that may never be answered. I have my own ideas in my heart about the man, and I have the stories from his friends and, most of all, stories from my mom. I also have more unseen, unreleased, and unknown items from the life of Elvis than most people can imagine. Each one comes with its own story attached to it.

Growing Up as the Prince of the King

My early memories of growing up in the Smith home were good ones. I had the good fortune of being adopted by family. They were the only parents I had known, and so it was easy to fit in. Music was a large part of my adopted dad's life, so he understood me. As soon as I started talking, I started singing. From all accounts, I still haven't stopped either of those two activities yet. Looking back, it must have been strange for the family to see me grow up. They had a front-row seat to see me grow and to watch the similarities to Elvis that I was starting to demonstrate. Another strange part of my growing up was that who I called Mom and Dad were actually my aunt and uncle. And that Aunt Gladys was really my grandmother, and I was her only grandson. Normal families have enough interesting dynamics all on their own without throwing someone like me into the mix. But in the mix I was. Imagine trying to get the second-generation Elvis to keep from following in his father's path when every indication is that he was born to perform. Apparently, they decided that there was no stopping me, so they settled for trying to direct me to a life of better choices than my father.

I can't help but wonder about something as I look back on my upbringing. Elvis and I were both raised in the Church of Christ denomination. One thing about this denomination is that while singing in worship is a vital part of the service, musical instruments are not a part of the service. In fact, musical instruments are not allowed in the church. This was a point that I debated during my tenure as a student at Grawood Christian School in Keithville, Louisiana, a Baptist school. The usual method to start a song during service was for the song leader to start the song in the proper key with a pitch pipe, and then the congregation would start singing. Usually in the wrong key, in spite of the pitch pipe. The official debate actually happened one summer day in Lubbock, Texas, at Lubbock Christian College. When I was fourteen, they started taking us to a preaching college to get used to the idea of becoming a preacher. I was comfortable onstage and sure liked to use my voice. Besides, ID was starting a school of preaching in Kingston, Jamaica, and he hoped that I might choose this direction. Maybe it was one more way that he thought that he could keep me from a life of getting into and causing trouble. After all, ID had spent years being a musician, and he knew the kind of things that were waiting for me out in the musician's world—a whole list of things to distract and tempt a young man and corrupt the virtues of my Christian upbringing.

I spent two summers in Lubbock, where they did the best that they could with me. One day in Professor Heinz's class, the debate came up about the use of musical instruments in church. My contention was that the Bible talks plenty about music, and especially when it mentions King David. Putting that aside, if we were going to ban musical instruments, then we needed to go all the way and get rid of the pitch pipe because the pitch pipe was a musical instrument. I was told that the pitch pipe is not an instrument as only one note is played on it to bring the congregation to the knowledge of how to sing the next song. I disagreed with the professor's assessment of my position. I attempted to prove my point further by pulling out my adopted dad's pitch pipe and playing "When the Saints Come Marching In." Do I need to tell you that this was not well received? I was pulled aside and informed that I would never pull a stunt like that again.

Here is another side note about the kind of things that happen over and over in my life.

Lubbock Christian College is one of the smallest and least-known schools in the area, much less in the country. Last year I moved into a house near North Scottsdale, Arizona. It is a small place out in the country, and I have a couple of neighbors living on the same land. I met my new neighbor Ron, and as we talked, he asked the usual question that I get asked. "Are you from Texas?"

I tell him, and he tells me that he went to college in Texas. I ask him where he went. Ron laughs and tells me that he can guarantee that I have never heard of it. He played baseball at a small Christian college in Lubbock. I start laughing and say, "Oh, you mean Lubbock Christian College." His jaw drops as I tell him all about it. I should be surprised, but I can't tell you how many times that this happens to me. I have started to expect this in my life.

Back to my thoughts about Elvis and the church. I wonder if my family tried to remove all the evidence of my parentage to protect me or to keep me from being linked to a man that became an example of everything that this denomination does not stand for? While Elvis grew up in the church and affirmed his faith in God, his life and lifestyle did not reflect the teachings and values of this denomination. Was Elvis considered to be an outcast of the church? I have a deep-seated faith and belief in God. I have also been rightfully accused of being irreverent at times. My debate that I mentioned earlier bears witness to this fact. I happen to believe that God made me with a sense of humor. I also am aware that I do not always use it properly. This does not change my heart and the way that I feel about the things of God. My question about Elvis is just a thought that I have. I have never asked anyone else about it. I am just curious how he felt.

Musical instruments may not have been allowed in the church, but they were in constant use in our house. Along with singing, I picked up the guitar and started to play at four years old. After a few years of being self-taught, my adopted parents hired a guitar teacher for me. After my fourth lesson, he told them to keep their money as I was already playing better than he was.

From the time I was old enough to be on stage, I was there. It became home to me. I felt the excitement of the moment and came to enjoy the creativity and even the spontaneity of live performing. I still thrive on spontaneity. Try to get me to stick to a set list for my performances. Go ahead, I dare you. If you do manage to get a set list on to the stage, I will guarantee you that it will not be followed. I will get an idea and deviate from the norm every time. I am not saying that it always works out like I intended, but it is the way I do things.

One such occasion happened on the last time that I played the Grapevine Opry in Grapevine, Texas, when I was ten years old. I did not intend for this to be my last time. It just kind of worked out that way. For every show at the Grapevine, there was a secret surprise guest. It was always a recognizable performer. Not always a star. It was someone who was a good performer and was actively working in the business. The owner of the Grapevine was Johnny High. He was notorious for sticking to his schedule. Changes and Johnny High did not get along at all. It made for a good tight show. After a while, even the band grew tired of this. As an artist, you are a creative person, and that creativity needs to be uncaged and set free from time to time. It just didn't happen at the Grapevine. It didn't happen until I showed up one night. The performers that were invited to perform sang two songs each, one in the first part of the show and the other in the later part. As I was getting ready to go on stage, I overheard who the guest artist was that night. It was Kenny Seratt, a singer that I liked, and he was here to promote his new album. There was a song from his last album that I liked. I had even sung it before at the Grapevine. I decided that I wanted to honor Kenny and sing his song for him while he was in the house. The fact that this would seriously mess with Johnny High was just a bonus. Keep in mind, I am ten years old. I am introduced as the next singer, and I climb the stairs onto the stage. As I walk on stage, I lean over to the guitar player from the house band and tell him that I am changing the song. He gets a wide-eyed look and tells me I can't. The band may not know the song. I tell him to relax, they know it. I tell him that it is Kenny's song and watch the realization of what is about to happen become a smile on his face. He turns to the band and gets them on board with it. He realizes that the uptight owner is about to have his show become spontaneous. The bandleader also knows that the owner of this song is backstage, and who knows how he will react to his own song being performed live. This is either going to be great or a real mess. Either way, the band will have a story to tell, years from now, and they have the best seats in the house to watch it happen.

My scheduled song and I were introduced, and I began to play and sing. Except I am singing a different song than is on Johnny High's scheduled playlist. I am watching the owner go out of his mind out of the corner of my eye. The band is loving it too. But wait. It gets better. As I am starting the second verse, out comes the surprise guest, much to the surprise of the owner. It is Johnny High's show. He is not the one who is supposed to be getting surprised. Kenny Seratt isn't due out yet. Kenny wasn't supposed to surprise the audience for a couple more songs. Kenny walks up beside me and joins right in. We finish the song as a duet with Kenny beaming at me, and the crowd was loving it. One of those spontaneous moments that turned out great. I almost always gain a new fan when I perform. This night, it turned out to be the artist that I set out to pay tribute to. As we walk offstage, he was telling me that he was just sitting back when he heard his song being played. It was the first time he had heard someone else sing his song. He was so moved that I chose to sing it that he had to join in. He was very appreciative and told me that I did him and his song proud as he thanked me. While we were wrapping up our conversation, the owner came offstage and was shaking his song list in my face. He told me that if I ever pulled a stunt like that again, it would be the last time I ever did. He kept going on about kids not knowing what they are doing until my new friend and fan raised a hand to silence the owner. He told him to hold on. He said that not only had I not done anything wrong, I had given a great performance, and it was the most fun the audience had ever had. Besides, we had already played the Grapevine, and there were plenty of places that we hadn't played yet. If the owner didn't like the way we did things, we would go play some of those other places for a while, and the owner could explain to the crowd why we were not coming back. What was I to do? Kenny had just stood up for me, so I chimed in and said, "Yeah. Me too." And that was the last time I ever played the Grapevine. At the ripe old age of ten, my Grapevine career was coming to an end. I did go out on top, and I kept the number-one rule of artists. Leave them wanting more.

Juilliard
and Hayrides

Performing on the Louisiana Hayride was one of the highlights of my young career. I did not think of it as a career at this point. I was just having fun. I did like the competing. Actually, I am not that competitive. I just really like winning. I enjoy the camaraderie of singers performing together. As a performer, I appreciate being in the presence of professionals practicing their craft. The Hayride was full of all of this. It had a heritage of great performers, including Elvis and my adopted dad. Countless greats and legends performed there. Winning Hayride competitions was quite a feather in my cap. It gave me a standard to measure myself by. I could compare myself to other winners and gauge my progress against theirs. More than anything though, I was having fun.

Then one day the Hayride seemed to take a backseat to everything. I am still not sure how it happened, but we got the call to audition at Juilliard. Looking back now, this was a big deal. At the time for me, it was a school. School and I did not see eye to eye. The classroom was not my friend. The classroom did not invite or encourage individuality or creativity. Even in music class, I was to be a part of the group. I was not free to be me. I was easily distracted, and I had a hard time focusing on anything that I did not consider to be important. My personality does play well with others. It just does not appreciate the finer points of a structured environment. Everyone else was thinking, "Wow! This was Juilliard. This was a big deal." I am sure that my adopted parents were excited about this opportunity. It is not that we were lacking opportunities for culture in the backwoods of Louisiana. I tended to be drawn to the more redneck side of life. I enjoyed being outdoors and playing with my friends. I grew up with some rather influential people who I only knew as my playmates. There were successful businessmen, people in the gas business. Other successful artists, such as Kix Brooks of Brooks & Dunn fame. As a teenager, I even came in contact with a group of guys that my friends and I admired. It was a local band named Sawyer Brown who was trying to get their break in the music business. They had a great sound, with Mark Miller singing lead for them. They eventually went on to great fame and, on their way up, were the winners one season on the television show *Star Search*. This was back before then. When we knew them, they were struggling to make it from gig to gig in the old school bus they drove, loaded down with all of them and all of their gear. One day they pulled into the gas station that my friend's dad owned. My friend worked there after school and on weekends. The boys from the band were counting out their money to see if they had enough to get them to their next booking. There are times in this business that you had enough money to get there, but you had better get paid because you sure didn't have enough money to get back home again. My friend and

I were watching them try to figure out how they were going to make it and deciding if they had enough money left over to eat before they got to their show. It is hard when you are so excited and passionate about pursuing your dream, and the ordinary things like gas and food seem to conspire to keep you from reaching your goals.

One of the things that I have never lost as I was growing up was the feeling you have as a kid. The feeling that you want to help anybody you see that is in a tough spot. We liked these guys and felt bad for them. The band finally decided how much gas they could afford, and we overheard the discussion that they hoped it was enough to get them where they were going. My buddy began to pump their gas. He and I never said a word, but we exchanged a look that said it all. They must have thought that it was taking a long time to put those few dollars' worth of gas in their bus. They didn't realize until they had pulled out of the station and headed down the road that they were experiencing a rare occurrence for a musician: a full tank of gas on their way to a gig. We used to limp into town on gas fumes and would fill up after we got paid that night. I remember watching Sawyer Brown on *Star Search* and feeling good. Feeling like we had a small hand in helping them one time. It was also good to see some good people get the recognition that they deserved.

I rubbed shoulders with several future famous stars. Another one took place when I was in elementary school. I was used as a human target by future Hall of Fame quarterback, Terry Bradshaw. At the time, Terry was in high school, and he already had quite an arm. He practiced on us. He was a nice-enough guy. It all changed when that football was in his hands. When that happened, he became one intense individual. When he was practicing on us, I don't think that Terry was working on his accuracy as much as his velocity. He sure seemed to get a kick out of it when his accuracy and velocity combined to dump us on our backsides. It was a moment of pride among my friends and I if we ever came in contact with a ball that Terry threw and managed to remain upright. Even more so if one of us hung on to the ball. The next best thing was if we could dodge the ball and make him miss one of us. Terry missing the target did not happen very often. This was all part of my life. It was a great time and place to be a kid.

I am sure that my adopted parents were so proud when the invitation came from Juilliard. Remember, they were in their forties when they adopted me, so they were more like proud grandparents. "What did your kids do this summer? My little Johnny went to Juilliard." Talk about the potential for bragging rights. With great anticipation, they loaded me up to go off to New York City, even though the place was full of Yankees. ID was so excited that he could hardly stand it. He kept telling me how to behave and how to greet people and to be sure that my shirt was tucked in. Sit up straight. Don't slouch when you stand. Try to speak clearly, we don't want them to think that we are uneducated hicks. He was never this nervous about any of my other performances. To him this seemed like the big time. If only we could land this one, then we would be set. I would have all the training and education that I needed. At this school they could channel all my excess creative energy into the proper directions. I was thinking something else. I was thinking, *School? In New York? They talk funny, and there is too much concrete. You can educate me all you want. I like being a hick. If that's what I am, then my friends must be hicks too. I like them, and we get on just fine.*

When we got to Juilliard, there was a very pleasant older gentleman, and he was very proper and refined. He gave me two pieces to sing that were some sort of classical songs. He told me that these would be my audition pieces. I looked at them, I really did. I wanted to make ID happy and please this nice man. I did look at the piece, and then I realized that there was no way on earth that I was going to sing this stuff. This was not me. No way, no how. I told the man that if he wanted to hear me sing the way that I like to sing and the way that I sing best, I would show him what I could do. He looked at me like I was the strangest thing that he had seen this week. ID was trying not to show how nervous he was. We were both out of our element here. I had traveled all the way here, and I was going to sing. I confidently stepped up to the microphone and busted out the song I wanted to sing, a very touching rendition of "Pistol-Packing Mamas." When I was done, there was silence. I determined that leaving someone speechless is not always the best thing. When the nice man regained his composure, he told me that he had never heard that song before, and it was very interesting. *Never heard that song? Where do these people come from? Don't they know good music? What kind of place is this anyway? What does he mean by* interesting? *They don't know "Pistol-Packing Mamas"? Everybody knows this one where I come from.*

Well, I get another try. The nice man tells me to go ahead and sing the other piece that he has prepared for me. I have other plans—imagine that. I decide to give these nice New Yorkers some culture of my own that they seem to be missing. I try again with another song that is just as popular. Again I am met with silence and a quizzical expression. I guess "I'm a Ding Dong Daddy from Dumas" is not on their playlist either.

It was shortly after this audition that I found out some useful information. There is a difference between being invited to Juilliard and being inducted. Being asked to visit does not mean that you get asked to stay at Juilliard. I used to tell people that I sang at Juilliard. As they were looking impressed, I would then ask them if singing in the parking lot counts. I guess that the good folks at Juilliard figured that I was already so good that they really couldn't do too much for me, and so they had better induct some other singer that needed the help, or something like that. At least that is how we decided that we would tell our story of our trip to the land of the big city. I was excited to get home. I had already had enough of this loud, dirty city. It was beautiful and exciting in its own way, but it was not me at the time. *Why would so many people live here when there ain't even any places to fish and they look at me sideways when I talk? They can shove their "school" up their butt. I'm going home. I'm sure that my friends have gotten a head start on causing trouble while I have been gone, and I can't wait to catch up to them.*

Back home and back to the Hayride for me. These were my people. I felt bad because ID wanted Juilliard so much. Later I wondered if he wanted it for me or for him. At his age, was he getting tired of trying to keep up with my ever-increasing curiosity and energy level? I didn't belong there, but it was nice to be invited. Knowing what I know now, I would be very excited about this invitation, should it happen again, but I haven't heard from them lately. Oh well, back to my people and back to where I love performing—on the Louisiana Hayride. In New York they have violins and cellos. As far as I was concerned, you can't even call it a real song if it doesn't have a fiddle and a steel guitar.

I did not realize at the time how much I was learning during the time that I spent on the Louisiana Hayride. From the time that I started performing, I always thought that I was good. From all reports, I had an innate ability to perform, to connect with an audience, and had an engaging stage presence. I did not understand that while my voice was good for my age, it needed to develop and be trained. I had all of the talents in their raw form and did not know enough to know that I needed to be groomed. I was born with it, and I thought that this was normal. It was natural for me. I had no concept that I should be groomed to get the most out of the talent that I was born with.

A funny thing was beginning to happen at the Hayride. As I began to sing around other performers, I did what most kids did. I started to imitate what I saw in the other singers. Without being formally instructed, I began to learn from those around me. The grooming was beginning to happen just by being around the professionals that I performed with. They acted like the professionals that they were and seemed to expect the same behavior from me. I saw what worked and what the audience liked. These were my early heroes and examples. I wanted to be like them and to act like them, so I did. It is natural for a young person to emulate what they see around them and to learn from their environment, especially if this environment is exciting and rewarding. Before long, I began to sound and act like I was much older than my young years would indicate. I will always be grateful for the experience that I received there. I also appreciate the other performers that influenced me. Most of all, I will always remember being a part of the great and colorful heritage and tradition of the Louisiana Hayride.

Lawrence Welk Is in Heaven

Growing up in a house full of women had many benefits. I seldom had to do much housework, and my performing schedule kept me from a lot of chores. There was one duty that I did have to regularly perform. Whenever a male escort driver or someone to carry the bags was needed, I was the one that was called on. I had turned sixteen almost a year before, and I was still at the stage of wanting to drive. It was a special privilege to get to drive at night. When my aunts wanted me to take them to go and see one of their favorite performers and his show, it was fine with me. They were excited to go see Lawrence Welk's show when it was traveling through and stopped at the Hirsch Coliseum in Shreveport. I was excited to get to dress up and go out. I was going to get to drive, and there would be good music and cute girls—two of the most important things in my world. There was no way I could ever imagine how those two things would come into play that night and change my life forever. We all put on our best clothes, and away we went to be entertained with an evening of singing and dancing.

I was raised by adopted parents that were basically the age of grandparents, so I was exposed to the older style of music. It surrounded me growing up. Because of this, I did have an appreciation for the style and the professionalism of Lawrence Welk and the show that he put on. I was also still a kid when I went to the show, so the snack bar held just as much appeal as the show that was taking place. I was amazed at one thing that I saw. Lawrence Welk was seventy-five years old. He was no spring chicken, but he was still rather spry. At one point he came down offstage to dance with a lady in the front row. When he came down to the audience seats on the floor, he was immediately mobbed by a hysterical gang of middle-aged women like he was a teen idol, and they were acting decades younger than their actual ages. Before we knew it, Lawrence had lost a shoe as well as one of the sleeves to his jacket. Who did they think he was, Tom Jones? The local police, acting as security, had to rescue him and escort him backstage, where he could change into a full set of clothes again. Music can be a dangerous business.

A little later in the show, I was feeling the effects of my trips to the snack bar, and I excused myself for a trip to the men's room. On the way back to my seat, I walked up a different aisle by mistake and found myself at the foot of a set of stairs that led to the stage. Lawrence Welk was standing at the top of the stairs and was beckoning me to come on up. I was not quite sure where I was or what I should do, but Lawrence was waving at me to join him. I could not turn him down. He was the star of the night. On the way up the stairs, this was feeling rather surreal. *What am I doing? I am in the middle of a show, and I am walking up the stairs to meet the star of the show. In the darkness, has he mistaken me for someone else? Does he think that I am part of the show?*

When I get to the top of the stairs, Lawrence is still smiling at me, so I keep going. I did not realize what was happening. This was the part of the show where audience members were invited up to dance with Bobby and Sissy, two of the most popular stars of the show. This is where I now found myself. On *Dancing with the Stars*, Welk style. I don't dance. I only do one thing onstage. I wonder what Lawrence was thinking when he saw this teenage boy standing in front of him. He told me that I looked a little young to know how to dance. What would I like to do on stage? I told him that I don't dance, but I do sing. I am not sure if he was asking me if I wanted to sing a song or if he was just asking to clarify that I did not want to dance. All I heard was the question that I always answer yes to. I saw a stage, a crowd, a microphone, and a piano player. I had everything I needed. I grabbed the microphone from him, and with all the confidence of a kid that does not know how big this moment is, I point at the piano player, and say, "I am going to sing 'Green Green Grass of Home' in the key of G. Hit it." It was one of my favorite songs by one of my favorite singers, Tom Jones. He was also one of my father's favorites, although I did not know it at the time. My father loved him as a singer and as a person. I had told Lawrence that I was going to sing, and sing I did. The crowd loved it. They were going nuts. I loved it too. There was yelling, screaming, and I received a standing ovation when I finished. I bowed to the audience and turned to hand the microphone back to a beaming and astonished Lawrence Welk. He shook my hand and patted me on the shoulder. He said something to me, but the crowd was still so loud that I could not hear a thing. I nodded a thank-you and headed back to my seat. I was trying to get back to my seat, and Mr. Welk was trying to continue with his show. Neither one of us had much success for a few minutes. It took a while for me to get to my aunts. I had to keep stopping to sign autographs and have pictures taken. Someone shouted out to Lawrence, "Why don't you hire him?"

Lawrence replied, "I think we will." It turned into quite a major disruption in the middle of a show, but Lawrence adapted like the professional that he was and kept the show going.

I finally made it back to my two aunts, who were so flushed with excitement that they could hardly stand it. They were as bad as the young girls that I had just encountered. They were talking in a mixture of excited squeals and matronly pride. They kept trying to act proper and act their age, but then the excitement and pride of what they had just seen got the best of them. They received instant recognition and status from their surrounding new best friends because they were with me. I had just made it back to my seat when I was tapped on the shoulder by a police officer. He told me that Lawrence would like a word with me backstage. My eyes got big, as my heart started to pound. This is not what I expected. I was being escorted by the officer when I spied John Timmerman in the crowd. He was waving excitedly at me. John was my adopted dad's best friend. I motioned to him to come with me. I wanted someone with me who can tell the world what happened to me if something goes wrong backstage.

John came along, and I was introduced to Lawrence. Three other gentlemen were there also. There was Stan Lewis, who owned Stan's Record Shop and Paula Records; Lon Varnell of Varnell Entertainment (Mr. Varnell was a talent agent that handled Barbara Mandrell); and the third gentleman was Sam Lutz (Sam was Lawrence Welk's agent).

Once we were all introduced and sat down to talk and I realized that this meeting was a good thing, I asked John if he could take my aunts home and let ID know that I would be a little late. By the look in his eyes, he was torn between staying and getting a firsthand account of what was happening before his eyes, or taking my aunts home and being the first one to tell what he knew so far. His chivalry won out, and he left us to see my aunts safely home. I could picture my aunts standing in the diminishing crowd, not knowing what to do, wondering how they were to get home. Their ride home just went backstage escorted by a police officer. I wasn't going to be coming back until they decided to let me come back.

One of the great things about youth is that you do not always know when to be intimidated when you find yourself as the odd man out in a group of highly successful professionals. I was still feeling the effects of the standing ovation I had received a short time ago. I knew what I had done to the crowd, and besides, they invited me here and sent a policeman to come get me. I was escorted like I was a star, and I felt like I was one. I sat up straight like I had been taught to do. I looked them in the eye, and I told them about myself. I told them my stories about the Hayride and the Grapevine Opry. Oh yes, I almost forgot. I was invited to audition at Juilliard. I talked about how I came from a musical tradition. How ID was on the Hayride too, and how he had sung with JD Souther and his band. This was the biggest thing that I had experienced. I was also on familiar turf. I was used to backstage. I spent a lot of time there. We talked, and I answered questions. Finally, Lawrence asked me the question. "What do you want to do?" I told him what I wanted. "I want to be the next Elvis." A simple statement and a simple goal. I want to be the greatest. What kid doesn't? Lawrence replied to me that he would have to see what he could do about making that happen.

Looking back on life, a lot of things make sense to you that you never see when you are living life in real time. I have often been asked, "Why didn't you? What happened? Why didn't you become the next Elvis?" The best answer that I have is that it was because of me. It was never an issue of talent. It was a question of how badly did I want it? What was I willing to give up for it? For someone to reach the absolute top, the pinnacle of their profession. Be it doctor, athlete, dancer, singer, CEO, whatever. They have to have a single-minded focus on their goal. It consumes them. It is all that they live, breathe, and dream. For the multitudes that never quite make it, sometimes their goal really does consume them, literally. Up 'til now, and probably even now, this has not been me. I love experiencing life. All of it. I am impulsive and multitalented. I will go off on a tangent if it captures my interest and my imagination. This is great for gaining new and broader experiences. It is not so good if your goal is to be the next Elvis. I may have missed being a global star, but I would not trade that for the life I have lived on my terms and the friends I have made along the way. I have more true friends than anybody I know in the music business. I know that they love me because I am me, not because I am an idol.

After Lawrence and I chatted for a little while more, it was then time for me to go. I was still on cloud nine and walking on air. I had started out the night being a nice nephew and taking my aunts to see their hero. I end up as the star of the show and getting personal attention from the man everyone else was paying to see. Not a bad night at all. The standing ovation was nice too.

I am reliving all the events of the night as I am making my way through the coliseum. Wouldn't it be fantastic to see my name on the marquee outside of an arena like this one? How would it feel to fill a place like this with my own fans, people that were paying good money to come see me? My thoughts were interrupted when I walked out of the door. I walked into the night and right into a crowd of young girls that were still waiting for me. They saw me and started jumping up and down and squealing. Holy cow, I have groupies. What do I do now? Talk about a deer caught in the headlights. I am just getting to the point where I like girls, but I am still kind of scared of them. I smile and wave and thank them. I slowly make my way through them, getting hugs and giving autographs on the way to my car. I was wondering if I was going to have any of them follow me home and how I would explain a parade of cars in my driveway.

By the time that I got home, I was the only one on the road, but I was not the only one still up. Everyone at home was still up and waiting. ID, Etta, my aunts, the maids, a few close friends. I was mobbed by them as soon as I walked in. I had to relive and recount each and every moment of the whole night, more than once, before they were satisfied. They were firing questions at me faster than I could come up with answers. While I was making my way home, they were busy making and receiving calls about what was going on. Etta had even made a list of all the people that had called and stopped by during that night and into the next day. And it was not over yet.

The next day, Lawrence Welk was quoted in the *Shreveport Journal* as saying, "I think Dennis is the best singer I've found in my lifetime. As you can see, even at my age of seventy-five, I've found this good singer, and I'm in heaven." This story was picked up by the local news stations and even made the New York and Los Angeles newspapers. The real kicker is that the next Sunday, I was written up on the whole back page of our church bulletin. That had never happened before for anyone.

A few days later, I heard from Lawrence again. He offered me a place on his show and wanted me to come to California to begin my training. Arrangements began to be made to bring me along as part of the Welk family. This was the start of the whirlwind for me. I was caught up in the days that followed and didn't even stop to think about the improbability of the events that had happened to get me where I now was. The coincidences are incredible. Looking back, I wondered if this was one of the coincidences that was really being orchestrated behind the scenes? I now see that this was one of many episodes in my life that I can't explain how or why— it just happens to me.

Before I could leave to go to the *Lawrence Welk Show*, I had to take care of a few things. I was only sixteen, so I had to get permission to leave school and make arrangements to take the GED. I also had to get written permission from my adopted parents. Lastly, I had to fulfill a commitment I made to a local school band.

We were going on a performing tour of several dates in Hawaii. It was a great time. We ended up playing almost all of the venues that Elvis played when he toured Hawaii. On the flight back from Hawaii, I was thinking about how it rained at the same time everyday. As I was lost in thought, the idea of a song came to me, and right there on the plane I wrote a song about a girl named Rhonda. It was called "Rainy Days I Don't Count, After You're Gone." Later we broke it up into two songs. We called one of them, "Don't Count the Rainy Days." You may have heard it. Not bad for a sixteen year old kid. When the tour ended, I left the group and stayed in Los Angeles. From there I started with Lawrence Welk.

Lawrence was there to welcome me to town after I got settled. He called me in, and we talked about what I wanted to do. I told him, and I also told him that I play guitar too. He raised an eyebrow as if to say, "This is even better yet." He asked me if I could show him. I could, and I did. Halfway through the song, I could tell that he was pleased. My time in California was starting out well. With my guitar skills, I was able to participate in numbers even when I was not singing. I could be a part of the band or provide accompaniment to another singer. This also made me the youngest singer/guitar player ever on the show.

Once again, this was another time of exciting new adventure for me. I was singing with new people from all over and learning from some of the best in the business. Two young men became my best friends on the show. They were the Otwell twins from a small town in Texas. They remembered me from when I walked on stage in Shreveport, and with all three of us being from Texas, we became fast friends. It was our first time away from home and our first time in a big city. We had a lot of fun and a few misunderstandings along the way. For the first month we looked like tourists, with our mouths wide open at all the sights. We were also informed that between Texas and Louisiana accents, we all talked funny. No one complained when we got up to sing though. After a while, we determined that we were beginning to fit in and that we were adapted to the Southern California culture.

The Otwells and I decided that it was time to try our hand at a popular weekend event. We headed south to Tijuana, a popular Mexican border town just south of San Diego. We spent the evening seeing the sights and bartering for deals. We were all still underage, even for Mexico, so we stayed away from the bars. Even though the bright flashing lights and swishing skirts of the young Mexican girls looked inviting, the fear of God that we all grew up with and the greater fear of answering to our parents one country and half the continent away kept us on the straight and narrow. Everything went relatively well until we were coming back across the border. One of the things that we did not know was that you don't drive to Tijuana. You park in the United States and walk across the border. From there you take a taxi. We were lucky enough to find the Suburban where we left it. It was still in one piece and still had the Texas plates on it. What we did not realize was how long it would take to get back across the border to our homeland on a Friday night. After what seemed like forever, it was our turn to be waved through. Except we weren't waved through. I guess that three young men in a big Suburban trying to cross the border in the middle of the night, with Texas plates, was considered worth a second look. The border guards wanted to ask a few questions of us. I was fine. I barely got a second look. A clean, fresh-faced, definitely Caucasian young man was not what they were interested in. Roger and David were another story. They both had dark tans and had started to try and grow beards to make them look older. This gave them a whole different look altogether from my innocent-looking face. I know that I am not the one being questioned, so I am just an interested observer. I might have been more nervous if I had realized the meaning of guilty by association. The border guard asked them if they were a citizen of the United States. They were having trouble getting their answer out for some reason. I don't know why. They are asked again by the border agent in a much more stern tone of voice. Their indignant response left me howling in laughter. "We are citizens of Texas." Leave it to Texans. We are Texans first, Americans second. It took a couple more repeats of this question before they got the answer right, and we were finally on the way home. I teased them all the way home about the United States of Texas. Hey, we were kids.

A couple of weeks later Roger, David, and I decided to make another trip to a local landmark. We wanted to drive down Sunset Boulevard and see what all the fuss was about and to see if we could see some movie stars. Again there was a Suburban involved. Our heads were on a swivel while we made our way down the boulevard looking at all the sights. I guess our driving must have been swerving like our eyes were. Our first indication of that was flashing lights from a police car behind us. We pulled over and made another cultural mistake. In Texas and Louisiana, when a cop pulls you over, you get out and meet him at the back of your car. You probably know him, and you visit a little bit and catch up on each other's families. He asks you about how your momma's doing while he writes you a ticket or gives you a warning. You also do it so that your friends can see who got caught as they drive by and honk and wave. In California, they do things a little differently. In California, when all three of you get out of the car and head to the rear of the vehicle, the officers draw their weapons and start yelling at you to lay hands firmly on your vehicle, like a Southern evangelist at a healing service. It took a few minutes for all of us to realize that we were from differing cultures. We finally sorted it out, and the officers became very friendly. They let us know that we should be careful in this part of town, and after looking us up and down again, they determined that we really didn't need to be in this part of town at all. I am sure that they could easily see themselves responding to our mugging call a short time later, so they encouraged us to make our way to another safer part of Los Angeles.

During this time, I had the privilege of getting to know Lawrence Welk better. He was an interesting man and definitely a class act. One of the funniest things about him was that he seemed to be more sheltered than I was. One weekend Lawrence asked me if I wanted to caddy for him at the Andy Williams Open, a golf tournament. He said that if I did, I could probably get to meet Andy Williams, and it might lead to a singing gig with Andy. I said sure, and the next day, off we went. I drove us down to the tournament in my car, an old Pontiac Bonneville with maroon velour interior. It was all the style back then. For the first few minutes of our drive, Lawrence kept surveying the inside of the car and finally asked how much a car like this cost. I told him how much, and he was amazed that he was paying me enough to own a car like this. I did not tell him that this was my adopted mom's car that they had given me so that I would have a good car out in California. ID told me I could have any car I wanted, but I did not want them to buy me a new car. I was just a kid. I was not sure which one I wanted yet. I did look longingly at the new Corvette, an official pace car model, before I made this decision though. It turns out that Lawrence had not bought a car for years. Dodge was one of his sponsors, and every year they sent him a new car, for free. He had no concept of money and how much things cost. It was an interesting contrast to the man that was so comfortable leading the band and who was so at ease in front of the television cameras. He had built a whole music empire and had the longest-running TV show going, and he did not know how to navigate simple areas of living day-to-day life.

We arrived at the tournament and met up with the rest of our foursome. Introductions were made, and off we went. Soon after, I decided that golf takes forever. At the end of eight holes, I was hot, tired, hungry, and thirsty. I had never caddied before and did not know what to expect. It seemed like we were walking for days. Lawrence spied a snack cart and asked if I would like a hot dog and a drink. Oh boy, would I! As we walked up to the cart, he was talking about what we both wanted to eat as he was hungry too. For a drink, Lawrence almost always drank milk. He had stomach issues that milk seemed to help settle down. As we drew near to the snack cart, Lawrence pulled a plastic coin holder out of his pocket and counted what was in it. He then ordered for us, but he only ordered something for me, and he walked away empty-handed. With curiosity, I watched him because I knew that he was hungry also. It dawned on me a moment later. Around the show there was much talk about how Lawrence almost never paid for anything. He was cheap, but not obnoxious about it. It was not that he refused to pay for things; he was seldom asked to pay for anything. He was famous, and people gave him almost everything that he needed. I realized that he hardly ever carried money and only had enough cash on him to pay for my lunch. I told him to wait for me for just a minute. I ran back to the cart and bought his lunch. I came back with his hot dog and milk and handed it to him. He was surprised and asked me how I had gotten it. I did not want to embarrass him and tell him that I, a young kid, had to buy his lunch for him. I told him that the snack cart guy recognized him too late and wanted to give him lunch in appreciation for who Lawrence was and what he did.

At the end, I did get to meet Andy Williams. He was very gracious, but I never sang with him. I ended up with a hot dog and sore feet and a sunburn to show for my day on the links.

As far as my own being sheltered, I had no idea who the others in our foursome were. I remembered their names but did not realize who any of them were until some time later. After all, none of these guys had ever sung a country song. How was I to know who they were? The other three members were Peter Falk of *Columbo* fame, Evel Knievel the daredevil, and Jack Nicklaus, who apparently knew something about playing golf. I guess I was not quite a man of the world just yet.

Back to Nashville... Twice

During a break from performing with the *Lawrence Welk Show*, I went back to Nashville and worked with HT on recording an album. Reggie Vaughn was the high school band director that sent me on the Hawaii tour. Reggie had introduced me to a friend of his down in Houston. His name was Lee Stuart. Lee had four songs that he wanted recorded. These songs were what I called cowboy music, songs of the Old West. HT told me that if I wanted to record an album, he would need some money to pay for studio time and to engineer the project. It was up to me to secure the funding and get Lee on board with the project. I am not sure if HT did not want to be bothered with it or if he was sending me out to talk to Stan to break me in to this part of the business.

I don't think that HT was taking it too seriously as I was going to lunch with Stan. HT sure was excited though when I called him after lunch. I had a check in my pocket for seventeen thousand dollars and a commitment for more to cover the rest of the production costs for the album. All of a sudden, we were really making an album. Again, I did not know enough to know that getting someone to fund a project is one of the hardest parts of getting started. People are usually long on ideas and inspiration and extremely short on cash to make it happen. My first experience at securing funding was to sit down at a lunch table and tell the man that we needed at least ten thousand dollars to consider starting the project. Without blinking, he replied with the seventeen-thousand-dollar check and wanted to know when I needed more. I excused myself from the table under the pretense of going to the restroom. I went to the pay phone in the lobby and called HT. I asked him, "What do I do now?" HT replied to my question as fast as he could, which wasn't all that fast. Hearing a Southerner try to talk fast can be an interesting event. They sound funny when they get excited. It is fun, even if you can't understand them.

"Take the money, Dennis, and get back here. No don't go to the casino! I don't care if you are feeling lucky, don't go to the casino! Dennis! Are you listening to me? I don't care if the check is made out to you. Don't take it to the blackjack table. No, Dennis, you do not get a commission on that check. Come back here now and bring it to me! Dennis? Dennis! Are you listening to me?"

I don't know why I get such a kick out of messing with people. Maybe it is because they believe that I am really capable of that much mischief. Maybe I do it because it is fun. Whatever the reason, I do it, and I enjoy it. I take the check to the waiting hands of HT. He made it sound like raising money was such a problem. This was easy.

Now we had the money. All that was left were songs. This was the real beginning of my songwriting and the whole process. This is my first encounter with the lyrics, music, recording, and working out arrangements with musicians. This was an album of cowboy music, songs that were full of lonely nights, starry skies, memories of lost loves, and hope for a better tomorrow. This album was full of vintage songs, of the Old West. I fell in love with the process of putting an album together. I ended up writing or cowriting all the songs on this album. Every day I would be writing, and I would work with whoever showed up to write with me. Some of the songs just needed to be completed. Some of them needed a whole rewrite. Others were written from scratch. The energy of all of this collaborative effort all focused on one project was intoxicating to me. I loved the long hours spent getting it right. I was surprised that I was taken so seriously. We wrote the songs in two weeks and then recorded the whole album in two more weeks. I did not know enough to know that it should have taken a lot longer. It was my first time, and I did not know what to expect. I just did what I did, and it happened that I have an ability to get the vocals to a song laid down in the recording studio in very few takes. I thought everyone did this. The musicians seemed to appreciate this, and I thought this was normal because they were getting their parts recorded with few mistakes. I did not realize at the time that the musicians and backup singers and even my producer had all worked with or around Elvis. They were the cream of the crop, among the best that Nashville had to offer at the time. HT was an employee and songwriter for Elvis. He stayed with Elvis in various capacities all the way until the end and, to this day, still carries on with people that were close to the King. This included a longtime working and personal relationship with Sherrill

Nielsen and the backup singing group the Jordanaires. Ray Walker, who was the leader of the Jordanaires, and HT are very close, personally and professionally, even to this day. To this day, HT still guides me in more than just music. He guides me in life, keeping the promise he made to Elvis about me and to watch me and watch out for me.

Having the Jordanaires in the studio with me was an awe-inspiring event. Again, this was my first experience on a project of this caliber, and I did not grasp how fortunate I was to be working with the best in the business. Even with that, I could tell that something special was happening.

I am still not sure why HT chose to point me in the direction of Western music. Was it just because that is what the investor wanted to pay for? Or was it something else? Why, with my talent, was I not appealing to more of a mainstream audience? After all, I was singing more mainstream, popular songs for my audiences in California.

As time has gone by, I realize that it may have been to keep me from the comparisons to my father. I was already being compared to Elvis on a regular basis in California. I did not pay it much mind. I took it as a compliment. I was also a kid and believed that I could be even better than Elvis. It wasn't ego. This is what kids do. We dream big and refuse to believe that there are limits on us and our abilities to achieve. When you are a kid, you do not dream of being second best. You dream of being number one. No kid ever dreams of being vice president or of being the backup to a star. For the most part, I shrugged off the comparisons to Elvis. He was the biggest thing around, and if someone wanted to refer to someone great, Elvis was the obvious choice. I had been receiving compliments about my voice since I was four years old. It was a nice compliment though, and I was pleased that people saw me this way. In the studio, there was a lot of talk going on behind the scenes about my uncanny likeness to the sound of Elvis in my singing. I was happy that these professionals were pleased with my performance. I had no idea that they knew firsthand what they were talking about. It was only years later, through the friendships that were forged and stayed true during this time, that I realized the magnitude and the accuracy of their comments and observations.

Ray Walker of the Jordanaires is one of these men. Ray has been and is today an inspiration and an immense talent, professionally and personally. His example and guidance over the years has been invaluable. I wish I could go back now and realize the importance of the mentors that I was blessed with at such a young age. From my adopted dad to HT, Lawrence Welk, Ray Walker, and Sherrill Nielsen, to name an important few. I grew up with royalty and didn't even know it. For my first album, Harold Bradley even wrote me a nice liner note. I later learned the magnitude of this. Harold was the president of the musicians' union in Nashville. He maintained that position for decades. In all his time as a musician and as union president, my liner note was the only one he ever wrote. This was and is something that I cherish.

When people hear my story, one of the many comments that I hear is that it was too bad that my father didn't leave me much of anything from his estate. It all depends on how you look at it. Did Elvis care for me and my mom financially? Yes, he did. He also gave me much more than that. He gave me something of even greater value. Men of character who Elvis trusted and worked with. Men to guide and teach me in my life and my career. Elvis could not be there, but he never left me alone. That is one of the most valuable things he could have left me.

Here I am. In the recording studio. Surrounded by greatness. And this is where I felt that I belonged. Every aspect of this process appealed to me. Thinking back on it now, my head is still full of the experience. It was a lifetime highlight that few ever get to experience. I was nineteen years old, and at the end of this process, I have an album with my name on it and memories of playing with some of the greatest musicians and singers ever. Not a bad start for a kid. A kid that is feeling all grown up. In my mind, I had arrived, and now I owned a piece of this town. It didn't seem that hard to me. Write a song. Play a melody. Record it, and do it again. I had plenty of songs in me. I didn't even mind giving some of them away. Other people could have them. I would just write more. I was kind of like Babe Ruth when he started playing baseball. After he hit his first home run, he said that hitting home runs was fun. He was going to hit a bunch of them. There is no realization that you are also going to strike out a lot too. Striking out was new to me. Success came naturally. And people wonder why I live life backward sometimes. At least it is backward from their perspective. It seems like normal to me.

The album was produced, engineered, completed, packaged, and was being sold. After some time went by, I asked HT when I would start to make some money off this cowboy album. HT laughed and told me that under normal circumstances, I would never make money on it. First, the investor gets paid back. I also failed to realize how much the record label took from a project. The label bills the artist for virtually everything. When an artist gets advance money for a project or gets paid for doing the album, it is not a payment. It is a loan. The artist has to pay the label back for every dime that they spend on him. The artist may get 20 percent of the royalties if they are lucky, and the label keeps the rest. Out of the 20 percent for the artist, he gets to pay 25 percent of that money for packaging of the album. He also gets charged for breakage of albums, for free samples that are sent out, and for all of the studio time, and the artist pays for the musicians and the engineering and mastering of the album. This leaves the artist making about one dollar an album on a good day. While all of this is going on, the studio sits back and collects their 80 percent, plus what the artist is paying for. You do the math and see how much of a windfall a recording contract can be.

This was a disappointing lesson and quite an eye-opener for me. It did not make sense to me. This was the first time that I was singing for a percentage, and I did not like the way it felt. HT wanted to let me know how the system worked, and it made me reevaluate my options. Why should a label make so much money off an artist? Sure, they provided the up-front money and marketed the product, but they had no product without the talent of the artist. I was not sure if I liked the way that this world was working. I liked the creativity of what we just did, but I found myself missing the regular paycheck of the *Lawrence Welk Show*.

During this time, I met a girl and fell in love. I had already developed a pattern in my life of falling in love a couple of times a month, as I was easily distracted by bright and shiny things. This was different though. I was feeling like I was growing up and had already seen lots of things. I thought that I was ready, and after all, she was Miss Tennessee and was very bright and very shiny.

We were in Louisiana and decided to go across the border to Texas to get married. We were in love and wanted to get married. Texas did not have the three-day waiting period that Louisiana and Tennessee had. I took two of my buddies along with me to be witnesses. The first judge that we saw ended up throwing us out of his courtroom because my buddies were goofing off and not taking this seriously at all. We had to rush to another county and get another license and act appropriately in the judge's chambers. We finally made it. Because of all the commotion, we did not have time to make all of the normal arrangements. As a result, we ended up spending the first night of our marriage sharing a room with my two witnesses. They were sleeping on the floor. The first night, my wife was spending the night with more than just her husband. I had no idea at the time how prophetic this night would turn out to be.

All of a sudden, being a grown-up meant that I had to go to work and support my new family. After a few writing jobs, I got a call from the Otwell twins out in Los Angeles. They were on the *Lawrence Welk Show* with me, and we had developed a good friendship. They wanted me to come back out to California and come back to the show. They told me that we could stay with them. They had a house that they were renting. It sounded like a good time and another new adventure. It was also better than anything that I had going right then. My new wife and I made the trip to California.

As fate would have it, shortly after we went to Los Angeles, the *Lawrence Welk Show* lost its television contract. After a few attempts at a new network, the show decided to fold up the tent and call an end to one of the most successful runs in the history of television. This left me far from home and out of work. What were we to do? Now this great idea of heading west did not seem to be panning out. Some of my impulses do end up this way.

We tried a few other things, but my heart was not in it. Up to this point, performing was my life, and now I felt like I was a king without a kingdom.

One day I had enough of California, and I called ID literally cold and lonely. I had taken my motorcycle and ridden up to Big Bear in the San Bernardino mountains. I was at the end of my rope. I was not where I wanted to be and wanted a change. I just did not know what yet. Possibly a product of growing up fast, away from family. I get that way sometimes. The pressure to always be "on" gets to you after a while. Being expected to perform for people and being seen as a commodity is new to me. I haven't learned the value of keeping life in balance and taking little bits of time for myself to keep my sanity. Since I started performing, I have grown used to pleasing people and bringing them joy. What I have not realized is that I was doing it for them, not for myself. I needed to find my joy in living. A friend of mine is a nurse, and she says of nurses that they give away to others what they most want to receive themselves. I think that to a degree, I am like that. I was having a great time, but the pressure and being away from family was getting to me. So my wife and I went up the mountains. It was snowing, and we were on the motorcycle that I bought when I sold my car.

I was used to Southern California beaches and was not prepared for snow. I kept riding because I love seeing new country and being out in nature. Also, the next adventure is always somewhere in front of me. The mountains and lake are beautiful. I will take off on a whim sometimes. My friends still joke with me that I am never the one that tries to talk anyone out of an idea. I am the one that says "Let's do it" and figure it out later. Well, now it is later.

When we got to Big Bear we found a place to stay up in the attic of a dog groomer's shop. We paid rent by cleaning the groomer's space. We helped out in the shop for grocery money. The owners would go down the mountain regularly, and that is when we were left to experience our current version of luxury. In the attic, we barely had a bathroom, and it was so cold that we got excited when our breath was not visible indoors. I am always trying to figure out something better than my current situation. My buddy says that he has to sift through one hundred of my bad ideas to get to a good one, but it is worth it to get to the one good one. It was time for a good one. We longed for a good hot bath and had no way of making it happen. That is, until I realized as I was cleaning up in the shop that there were some really big metal tubs that we used to wash the dogs. I gave them an extra good scrubbing and started heating water. I called my wife downstairs and said one of my most often used phrases: "You are not going to believe this." It may have looked like an Old Western movie, but it felt like heaven. It was so good to be clean and toasty warm. We did not even mind when our fingers got all pruny from being in the water for too long.

We made do up there for a while. We were stuck. There was just enough to survive up there on the mountain, but never enough to get us back down to civilization and our friends. Besides, I wasn't sure what I would do if I could get back down there. I am stuck and tired and cold. I miss my family, and I miss Southern life. I long for something familiar in my life. Then one day, the owners of the business left and did not come back. After a couple days, people started coming around looking for them, and I could tell things were not good. We were about out of groceries, and I knew we weren't going to get paid any time soon.

This is when I called home, and my adopted dad got in the truck and drove to get me up in the mountains. I was never so glad to see him. As an indicator of his character, there were no lectures—just a warm truck, a shoulder to lean on, a listening ear, and the comfort of the familiar. We had a lot of long conversations on the way to the airport. One of the great things about my adopted dad was that he understood what makes me tick. He did not try to change me. He didn't tell me to act normal. I was not compared to other children that behaved in the usual manner. He understood that with my talent comes a trade-off. It is seldom that you find a person with an unusual talent who is well-rounded in all areas of life. It is like the talent steals energy or ability from other areas in your personality. I don't know if this is to keep you grounded and humble or if it is just a law of nature. Maybe God realizes how dangerous it is to your soul, to be completely caught up in yourself and what you can do. Whatever the reason behind it, I know this about myself. ID knew it too, and it was nice to have someone close to me that understands. I can also be just Johnny to him. He knew me as a person, not just as a performer.

Once I was back in the familiar world of home, we talked and made plans to go to Nashville and continue working with Harrison Tyner (HT). This began my stint with Adonda Records as one of their featured artists.

My adopted dad had paid for my recording time and for HT to produce several new songs for me, which years later would become part of an album. I still needed to eat and live while all this was going on. I got a job writing songs for Adonda. It was not glamorous at all. At times I felt like I was churning out romance novels that all had the same formulas. Every once in a while, I would have a song that was special though. This made it all worthwhile. To paraphrase Bono from U2, the music business is like a coal mine—dark and dirty and disappointing, but you keep going because once in a while you find the diamond. This one song was one of my first diamonds. This is the story of this song and of one of the many people that I have met along the way.

"Isn't it awfully late for you to be out? What are you working on?" I looked up as the older man sat down. There was barely enough room on my small table at the Pancake House in Nashville for me, my oversized chef's salad, the list of daily meal specials, and my writing pad. This is one of the places that I come to write songs when I need a change of scenery, some privacy, and a meal I can afford. It is open all night, and the chef's salad is big enough for two and a half meals. For $4.95, it is a good deal, no matter how you look at it. Especially for a young guy trying to make it.

I look across the table at my uninvited dinner companion in annoyance as I move my stuff out of the way. It is four in the morning, and I thought I would be writing in privacy. Oh well, my adopted dad taught me to respect my elders, and I'm nineteen years old, so everyone looks older to me. I'm nineteen but look fifteen, and this kindly man is probably wondering what a young kid is doing out by himself at this time of night. He asks me what I am doing, and I tell him that I am writing.

"Are you a musician?" he asks.

"I am a singer and a writer, but I do play guitar too."

"What are you doing here in Nashville?"

"I am recording and doing some writing."

"Are you recording demos or cutting songs?"

"I'm cutting songs over at Adonda Records with HT, Harrison Tyner."

"Really?" he asks with eyebrows raised and head cocked to the side. He seems to be taking another look at me and wondering what the back story on me might be.

"Do you have a band or musicians that are working with you?"

"We have a bunch of pickers. Harold Bradley is leading them." Now Harold Bradley is a known name in town.

At the mention of Harold's name, my tablemate leans back and takes an even longer look at me. He seems to be thinking, *How in the world did this wet-behind-the-ears teenage kid swing this deal?*

My new friend takes a different approach. "What are you working on there?" he asks, motioning to my notepad.

"It's a song about my grandpa. I am kinda stuck. I never knew him and don't know where to take the song from here."

"Well, you have to live it before you can write it," he says.

"Oh, I have lived it." I smile now at the thought of me making this statement at my young age. Compared to my friends, I have lived a lot already. If only I had known.

"Really? You have lived it? What are you, fifteen?"

"No, sir. I am nineteen years old, and I have seen a lot already."

After this, we spend several minutes just talking. My new friend finally gets up to leave, and before he does, he takes out a card. He writes his phone number on it and tells me that if I ever have a song that I would like to get out there, I should give it to him. He would take a look at it. I thank him and turn back to my work.

I am still staring at my half-empty notepad as the waitress is hurrying over to my table. What now? This quiet workspace is turning into a busy office. The waitress exclaims to me, "Do you know who that was sitting with you?"

"No. I never even saw him before. Just a guy in a baseball cap in the middle of the night."

She is standing there looking down at me dumbfounded. "Well, he paid for your salad." She was waving the ticket in my face.

"That was nice of him, but I still don't know him."

The waitress finally found her voice again and stammered out, "Look at the name on the ticket! That was Kenny Rogers!"

"Really? Wow. I guess I sound even more foolish now."

It was great to meet him and talk with him. I wish I had known it was him. He was the last person I expected to meet in the middle of the night in an all-night coffee shop. Oh well. I have some songs to write. I have to get new songs out every week for the songwriting group that I am working for. Most of the songs aren't much good. Just a bunch of young guys writing songs, pretending that we know about life and love and loss. We don't get credit for our work. It belongs to Adonda, a subsidiary of Capitol Records, but at least I get a regular paycheck. That is a rare commodity in Nashville. Sometimes you have to trade in your creative genius for the credit of others in exchange for regular meals and a bed.

I finally finish the song I was working on when I met Kenny, and I decide to take him up on his offer. I make a demo of my song and e-mail it to Kenny. Oh wait, we don't have e-mail yet. I make a cassette recording (remember those?). Now I am faced with the monumental task of getting past the front desk of the office where Kenny is. Ironically enough, when I asked someone about how to find Kenny Rogers in this town, they laughed and told me to go to the Quonset hut that I work in, walk out the front door, and keep walking straight across the street into the office building. Kenny had recently set up shop across the street from my work. At this point, I am still taking the word of a midnight waitress that it really was Kenny. I am not sure if it was charm, pity, or desperation that got me past the receptionist, but get by her I did. I made it to a secretary in the back. She looks me up and down and asks me if I would like to present a song.

"Yes, ma'am, I would. I have this cassette here with a song on it. I want to get it to this man," I explain as I pull the card I was given out of my pocket. "The waitress at the Pancake House says that it is Kenny Rogers, but

I don't know. He just gave me this card and wrote his number on it."

The secretary looks at the card and looks at me again with a whimsical smile, knowing that I have no idea how close I was to greatness that night in the diner. She smiles again and informs me that yes, that really is the number to Kenny Rogers, and she will see that it gets to him. I thank her and make my way out of the plush office building and back across the street to the hut that I am working in. Maybe one day, I will be in the nice office and have a secretary to take care of me.

I never heard back from Kenny, but my boss did. My boss was pretty happy about it. You see, that song that I wrote, it was called "The Old Man in Our Town," and it was the B side of the record "You Decorated My Life," which was one of Kenny's earliest big hits in country music.

This is just one of many chance encounters that have touched my life. Funny thing is that I don't believe in coincidence. I do believe that God has a plan for my life, and I was just starting to find out what it is. I had just gotten to town and already had a famous producer/manager. I had the most famous musicians in town playing for me, I had the most famous backup singers in town, and I had just written a song for Kenny Rogers. Not a bad start for a young man in Nashville.

It was during this time that I met Steve, Rudy, and Larry, three brothers that you know as the Gatlins. In Nashville, there were only three places that we ate, and I started to notice that wherever I went, one or three of these brothers always seemed to be there. Being me, I haven't met a stranger yet, so I had to go meet them.

Rudy and I became instant friends, and shortly after that, we all started writing, performing, and causing trouble together. With each success, we were becoming more sure of ourselves or, as other people put it, cocky. One night we finally went too far. Rudy and I were at Cactus Jacks, telling each other stories and toasting ourselves and each other's successes with a few adult beverages. We were sitting there with HT and a few other key people in the music business. We were having a great time until a gentleman named David Briggs spoke up. He informed Rudy and me that we had grown too big for our britches and that Nashville and all concerned would be better off if Rudy and I would take ourselves to Texas for a while and learn to grow up. He was of the mind that we were too young to be having such success.

We could not believe our ears. Here we were, having a great time and enjoying our success. We could not comprehend that other people had been struggling and trying to get their break since before we were born and were still trying to make it up to music row. Who was this guy to be telling us what we could and could not do? I was in the process of getting up and getting in David's face so I could show him that I was not intimidated by him or what he had to say to me. An older man sitting next to me placed his hand on my arm and told me to sit down. This was not the time or the place. He patted my arm and attempted to reassure me and calm the situation down. Rudy and I were still pretty mad about how we were being treated. We got up to leave and didn't care how loud we were on our way out the door. Youth trying to draw attention to themselves to hide our inexperience.

Rudy and I decided to show David how grown up and mature we were. We would give him something to think about when he next thought of mouthing off to us. So we went outside of the bar and keyed his car and flattened all four of his tires. Now we will see who's all grown up. We even scratched our own names in the paint of his car to show him that we did indeed know how to write. In fact, we could even spell correctly too.

This was Saturday night. Monday morning we get an invitation to meet at the Capitol Records office. Have you ever received an invitation that was not really an invitation? It wasn't even what you could call a request. A nice way to put it is that we were informed that we would be attending a meeting immediately, if not sooner. Once at the office, we were directed to a room where we were given a history lesson. Recent history, but an important history lesson, nonetheless.

Lesson one: It seems that recently, Jim Reeves had passed away. Jim Reeves was music royalty. He was untouchable. He really did own a piece of the town and also helped make country music what it was. Upon his passing, Jim Reeves's widow had given his favorite car to one of Jim's best friends and collaborator. That car was both expensive and valuable for several reasons, including sentimental value and bragging rights around town. HT was very proud to have received it. HT had loaned it to one of his good friends, David Briggs, who was just as proud as HT, and he drove it with great pride. At least until Saturday night, when two young men decided to display their writing talents for all the world to see in the paint of this car.

Lesson two: We were invited, much like our first invitation of the day. Okay. We were informed that we would be going to Texas after all, to learn to grow up and maybe to mature just a little. Evidently, good penmanship is not rewarded in the real world like it is in school. Nothing cements a friendship like two young men sharing a punishment. We have laughed about how foolish and just plain dumb we were many times over the years.

The funny thing is that this story just came up again twenty-nine years later. I was playing for a group of people in an informal setting in a lounge in the Phoenix area. The group was a mix of cowboys, locals, and the well-to-do. After I was done, I was visiting with my new friends. It always seems like I meet a dozen new friends every time I play. During my set, I did a medley of the Gatlin brother's songs, and a well-set-up and proper lady was commenting on those songs. She informed me that she was on the board of a charity and that the Gatlins were in town to perform at the charity. I replied that I knew them and had sang and toured with them. I told her that Rudy and I especially were good friends and asked her if he was there too. She looked at me like, *who did I think I was?* I was obviously dropping names and trying to one-up her. I told her that I did know him. I had known him for at least thirty years. I said, "In fact, I will prove it to you. If you are the one that is setting up this charity event as you claim, then surely you have a number to get hold of Rudy. Call him, and I will talk to him for you. I would love for him to come over, and we can play and sing a little for all you good folks." I then turned to the crowd. "Wouldn't all you fine folks like to have one of the Gatlins here?" Well, now she is on the spot. Her husband is grinning like the cat that ate the canary. He is loving every bit of watching his wife squirm. He is also measuring me to see if I am running some scam or if I am for real. He decides that either I am for real or that this is going to be a lot of fun, no matter how it turns out, and urges his wife to make the call. She does so hesitantly after protesting that she does not want to bother Mr. Gatlin. She reaches Rudy's assistant. She timidly asks that if it is not too much trouble, could Mr. Rudy Gatlin please call her back. Two minutes later, the phone rings, and her eyes get huge. She says hello, she identifies herself, and she apologizes for bothering him. It seems that there is a man here that would like to speak to him. She tries to hand the phone to me, and I stop her. I tell her that I don't want her to think that I am trying to pull anything over on any of them, so will she ask Rudy one question for me. She asks, "There is a gentleman here that has been singing for us, and he wants to know if you remember Cactus Jacks?"

Rudy's voice comes booming back through the phone, "Aw, hell! Is Johnny there?" The place erupts with hoots and laughter. Rudy and I have a nice chat, and we hang up with a promise to speak the next day. Once more, don't doubt Johnny. Like a good reporter, I try not to ask a question that I don't already know the answer to.

The Texas Years

Ah, Texas. Land of my birth. Where everything is bigger. This was a great time of adventure for me. I was learning a lot and finding out even more. I am naturally trusting in people and am always looking for the best in people. In California I learned about people that would smile and shake your hand and pat you on the back. What you didn't know was that the hand that was patting your back was also holding a knife, in case it was to their advantage to stab me in the back and advance themselves. In Texas, it was open season. It was also full of Southern hospitality, and a handshake and your word meant everything to a whole lot of people. My people. This was a time of working with bands and learning to work the crowds. It was a great time of performing, writing, and seeing a state that I love. I made lifetime friends during this time and also saw the effects of choosing your friends poorly. In one case, I watched my band manager go to jail for financial impropriety.

My years in Texas came after some personal events that were very hard to experience. While in Nashville, I had experienced a lot of growing up. This growing

up had been delayed as a result of being a child star on a small scale. When you display unusual talent as a child, be it acting, singing, or sports, people treat you differently. I am not saying these things to say that I deserved them. It is just the way that it is, right or wrong. It is how the world works. You are catered to as much as a child can be catered to. There are people that want to be around you, so they try to make life easier for you. People want to be recognized by you and to be seen with you, so they do things for you. A basic desire in a person's life is that they want to be noticed.

My adopted dad was more like a grandparent than a parent in this regard. He wanted me to focus on grooming and expanding my music opportunities, so I bypassed some of the lessons of life that a young man lives along the way. I try to imagine what must have been going through his mind. He was raising the son of a superstar, and he was responsible for pointing me in the right direction. He would also hold himself responsible if I went off in the wrong directions. When Elvis was growing up, he was the son of a common man. If Elvis had met with mild success or had just been a good soldier in the army, nobody would have said that Elvis missed his mark in life. Instead, Elvis made a huge mark on the world, and now eyes were on me and on my adopted dad to see if I would become something to the world. Or would I be like the vast majority of musicians with a small following and a full-time job to support myself, with music as a hobby?

Some of my late growing up is also a part of me. I am still waiting to see what I will be when I grow up. I look at the world differently than a lot of people. There are signs and embroidered sayings all over that talk about living in the moment. These sayings talk about it. I do it. I am sure that if the sayings were longer, they would talk about living in the moment and, during the process, finding balance in your life. Most people have to learn how to live in the moment to get some balance in their lives. I live in the moment every day. It is how I am put together. As Lady Gaga says, "I was born this way." For me to achieve balance in my life, I have to consciously learn to be concerned about what tomorrow and next week brings. My natural tendency is to enjoy today, with little regard for tomorrow. It is a lot of fun. At least until tomorrow or next week shows up. I don't always consider the consequences of what today's actions will bring next week or next month. This is one of the drawbacks in my life. I know who I am, and overall, I would not change my life and how I am. I have learned to like my life and who I am.

The last few years in my life had brought quite a bit of growing up and had brought it fast. Some were good, like writing songs and recording an album. Some other things were not as good. These were experiences that I could have done without. Growing up, I learned a lot about music but missed out a lot on lessons about life. So one divorce and one annulment later, I was back in Texas. These stories are not easy to tell and are for another time. The divorce, I will address later. The annulment, I will chalk up to a mutual mistake. Pardon me if I skip over some details now. Out of respect for myself and for others that have been in my life, I need to consider personal privacies in some areas.

So here I am back in Texas. I am living off money from recordings and songwriting. I have a nice condo to live in.

I am driving a nice car. I have no daily responsibilities. I am learning to enjoy life and am getting over some of my recent heartbreaks. I am on my own and have no one to make happy or to report to. For a time it is a good life. For a time… Then the other part of me starts to kick in. I need the stimulation of moving forward. I am energized by the prospects of something new. I have so many interests in life and in business that my eyes are open to everything. This is where I believe God's hand keeps stepping in. The doors keep opening to music—over and over.

I am talking to a friend of mine. She invites me to a party. We are just friends. She tells me that there is a man that is in the land title business and loves music. He has a lot of money and wants to manage a musician. I was to attend the party as her date, and she would introduce me to Bill Perry. At the party I get introduced, and after Bill has a few more drinks, he asks me for the third time if I can really sing and if I know any songs. If I do, how about I get up onstage with the band that is playing and show him what I can do. Here I go again. One more time. This is not the first time and will not be the last. I do not make a big deal about my abilities and what I can do. I tell them that yes, I can sing, and yes, I really can play guitar. People tend to feel like I need to show them in order for me to prove myself. They usually want me to get onstage so that they see for themselves whether or not I am just another bad karaoke singer with big dreams. So one more time I get onstage and sing with the house band. I do one song, and then it's on. When I get up and do a song, I try to be respectful of the band that I am now singing with. I am interrupting their moment, at someone else's request, and I know how that feels. I am not fond of other people walking onto my stage and interrupting me while I am working. I don't want to show them up. They are working hard to entertain us. I join them in one of their songs that they are singing and sing with their singer. Ninety times out of a hundred, it works out great. The band and I bond onstage. We have some great times and sing a few more songs together. They recognize my professional abilities, and we have mutual respect for each other. Occasionally, someone gets offended or insecure in these situations, and I excuse myself graciously and sit back down in the crowd. This time it went well. I ended up singing for the rest of the night with the band. Bill Perry was so excited that he couldn't wait for the next day to start making plans with me.

Within the week, we formed Excelsior Music and decided to build a band around me. Here I go again. What about HT and Nashville? Was I ignoring him? HT and I had a great relationship during these times. He and I talked almost daily. HT took the position of letting me know that he was there if I needed him for anything and would support me in any way that he could as I did my own thing. Now it was time to build the band and start writing songs. We put together a great band and started rehearsing cover songs while we were working on new and original songs. We named the band Southern Thunder. This was just what I needed. The creative juices were flowing. We started out on the road, playing where we could and building a name for ourselves. Before long, we were selling out venues, and honky-tonks. Recording an album is an amazing experience, but the reward comes later. Playing in front of a live crowd and feeding off their energy is an intoxicating experience. You feel an immediate rush as they respond to you, and you hear them singing your songs along with you. We were getting such a good response that we made an album that we could sell at our shows, and we also had shirts, hats, and ladies underwear made up, all of them with our band logo on them.

After one more successful road trip, I came back to Dallas, and Bill Perry presented me with a Rolex watch, and he asked me what it would take to make his singer happy. I told him that I wanted a red Cadillac Allanté parked out front in the morning. Sure enough, the next morning when I got to the office, there it was. Bright, shiny, red, brand-new, and mine, all mine. Or at least I thought it was all mine. I was convinced that I was on top and would always stay there. One night a short time later, Bill Perry and I were out at a bar. Somehow or another, I turned my arm, and my Rolex watch cut my wrist. I took it off and held it in my hand while I rubbed my wrist where it had been cut. Bill Perry saw that my watch had cut me. He swore and grabbed it out of my hand. He then threw it across the room as hard as he could with another expletive. It slammed against the wall, next to the stage, and shattered to pieces. He looked at me and told me that with his money and my talents, we could buy hundreds of those watches. People often wonder why I don't have a huge regard for material possessions now. I have already had them. I have had large houses, new cars, expensive jewelry, big boats. I know what those bring. They are nice, but they don't change me into a different or a better person. They also cannot cover up what is missing on the inside of a person's life.

There were many great things about this time. One of the best things was that nobody in the band knew me. They only knew the history that I shared with them. As a result, they accepted me as an equal or even better. I was part of the music group and the first one to be there, so I had seniority, even though I was still pretty young. I was also writing a good portion of our songs. I had instant credibility and a fresh start. This felt good to me. I had no history here and nothing to prove. It was also Texas, and we had a lot of fun, onstage and off. Everything is bigger in Texas.

One night we were scheduled to perform for the Toastmasters convention. We were opening up for Asleep at the Wheel. That day, we found out that the headliner's bus had broken down, and they were scrambling for a replacement. It turned out that Alan Jackson was close by, and so they scheduled him to fill in for Asleep at the Wheel. Just before we went on, they thought that Asleep at the Wheel would be able to make it after all, and they already had Alan Jackson committed also. They told us to go on and do our normal set. They were just going to give the audience an extra treat, with three groups playing that night. Our set was going great, and the crowd was into it. Halfway through, we were told that Asleep at the Wheel was not going to make it after all. Alan Jackson was not scheduled until later, so we would have to keep playing. Tell a band having a great night and a great audience that they get to keep playing, and most times they will keep playing for free. We told the crowd that we were going to be with them for a while longer, and the applause was thunderous. We were having a blast. I was on that night. I have been told that I am pretty good on an ordinary night, but I have to tell you, that even by my standards, this was a good night. And the band was so tight. They were in the groove. It was like we all knew what the other people were going to do before they did it. It finally came to an end. We were exhausted and grinning and out of songs. We had already started playing other people's songs, and we couldn't play any of Alan's hits; he was up next. The audience gave us a great send-off and welcomed Alan to the stage. Compared to us, Alan must not have had as good of a night. He put on a good show, but I don't think he was used to such a good opening act. As Alan walked offstage, he grabbed his manager with one hand and my manager with the other. He told them both in no uncertain terms to never ever let that band open for him again. He then kept hold of his manager as he walked off, and we heard him telling his manager to never do that to him again. We like Alan, but we were grinning even more. It was further proof of how well we did that night.

We kept going, and our popularity and stage shows kept getting better. It was busy and demanding, but I was having a blast. I love being in front of an audience, and the band was a great bunch of guys to be on the road with. We had gone into the studio to cut an album, and then we were back on the road. Until everything changed. They say in Texas that if you don't like the weather at that moment, wait just a little; it will change. The same holds true for the music business. You can go from top to bottom or bottom to top very rapidly. It is more often top to bottom than the other way around. I was back in town for a few days in Dallas. Big Jim, an accounting guy, came by and asked if I was free for lunch. I told him, "Sure. Hold on, and I would get Bill Perry to join us." Bill and

Jim were friends. Jim held up his hand to stop me and told me he wanted to see me alone. This was not a good sign. I better see what Jim wants.

We go to lunch, and over lunch, Jim tells me about an ongoing investigation into the financial affairs of Bill Perry. Jim tells me that Bill has been kiting funds to the tune of thirty million dollars and has been using the music business as well as his land title business as a front to cover up his activities. I have had some bad lunches, and this one was one of the big ones. Jim wanted me to know because he did not want me to get caught up in the mess when Bill went down. Jim knew that I had been there since this venture started and wanted me to be sure that I would have no legal ties to Bill's illegal activities. I did not, thank God. I just wanted to sing, and Bill kept telling me that I would own part of all of this, but I had never seen any paperwork to make that happen. Everyone assumed that my name was connected to Bill's, and I was going to have to figure out how to keep myself from going down with him. Now, how was I supposed to work my way out of this one? I am way too pretty to ever go to jail, so I was eager to remove myself. How to do it though?

My friends tell me that if I ever get arrested, by the next morning, the sheriff would be working for me. I just seem to have that knack of falling down and ending up in a better situation. Here I am wondering how to get out of this deal when I get a call from Bill Perry just a few days later. He wanted me to meet with him and his attorney. His attorney had a contract for me to sign. When I came to the appointment, they presented me with a contract for me to sell them some of my songs. I did not know a lot about contracts, but this one looked bad. After you have been screwed a few times, you start to recognize some of the signs, and you learn what to look for. With a noncommittal expression, I told them that I wanted to read it before I signed it, and I would get right back to them. Suddenly, the attorney started to sound like a salesman telling me that this offer was only good for right now, and they would not be this generous if I did not sign it now. I told him to just hold on. As an attorney, was he advising me to sign something that I did not understand? Could this be construed as misleading or malpractice? At these questions, the attorney settled down.

I told them that I would be down the hall, and I would let them know when I was done. I knew my way around the office and went straight to an office with a fax machine in it. I was still in contact with Harold Bradley, the president of the musician's union in Nashville. I sent him the contract to confirm my suspicions of how bad this contract was. About the time that Harold received the second page of the contract, my phone rang. It was Harold. Harold told me that he was not sure where I was or what I was doing or what I was up to, but he said to run not walk away from them and from this deal. If I signed this contract, I would be working for free for the rest of my life. My kids would probably end up owing them money.

I went back to find Bill Perry and the attorney. When I found them, I told them that this was a big deal. I had a lot on my mind and that I would have to think about this for a few days. I left out of there to go perform a local show that night.

A few days later, the band and I were to perform at Borrowed Money, a club in Lubbock, Texas, owned by

Sonny Bird. Sonny also owned a local strip club and a bail bond company. Sonny was a real entrepreneur. He let us all know that if we ever needed to spend some of the money he paid us in either one of his other businesses, he would be glad to help us out. Fortunately for me, I never had a need for any of his other services. At Borrowed Money, we were the headline act on the main stage. There were three other opening acts. They were Leroy Parnell, Restless Heart, and Toby Keith.

It was the first time that I had met Toby. He had just gotten his first bus. When you get to move from the van to a bus, it is considered a big step for an artist. I was not quite sure about this step for Toby though. His bus was just a hull with no amenities. I stepped inside, and I saw two things: a couch and a weight set in the very back. It was a bus and not much else. This was part of the beginning of Toby Keith. He was one hard worker. He was grinding it out on the road, trying to make his dream come true. A few months after this, I was pulling into another engagement where Toby was playing, and as we pulled in, I saw Toby underneath his bus. He was working on his own bus. He is a warrior when it comes to doing whatever it takes. While he was on the road, he would spend the days in the recording studio working on his new material, and he spent his nights onstage. It was nonstop for Toby. He has earned every bit of his success. He earned it the hard way.

After seeing Toby's first bus, I did not have the heart to tell him that I would be flying back to Dallas in a private plane later that night. We were milling around and meeting each other and trading lies about how big our crowds were, how bad our venues were, and how beautiful the girls were. Normal stories from the road. While this was going on, this long-haired fellow approached me and introduced himself as the bandleader and drummer for Restless Heart. They were opening up for us. Their group used a lot of harmonies in their songs, and they had a nice sound. I was still laughing at the drummer being the bandleader. The old line in music is that you don't marry a drummer. You bring the drummer home to scare your parents so they will be happy that you are dating the guitar player.

He really was the bandleader. I was informed that the lead singer was leaving the band to go try his hand at a solo project with Capitol Records. The drummer wanted to know if I knew their songs and if I would want to consider finishing the tour with them as the lead singer. I told him that I did know their songs and I was interested, but I didn't let him know how interested I was. I told him that it was a possibility, and I would let him know shortly. He didn't realize how shortly it would be. He had approached me because he had heard some rumblings about what was going on with me and Bill Perry from my own band members.

In the previous few days, the word had gotten out to my band about the deal that I had been offered with Bill Perry, and there was a lot of talk that I would not accept this contract. The band was worried about what would happen to them if I left. They would need a new singer in a hurry if they had any hope of sticking together. Bob Williams, our drummer, had heard of this guy named Ty Herndon, who was trying to get a band together and get some backing. There are two things that are almost always going on in a band. Some sort of unrest about who is not happy and gossip about it. There are no real secrets. The problem was that we could all keep secrets. The people we told the secrets to, they couldn't keep them. The talking that was going on behind the scenes was no big deal in itself. It was a part of band life. The band did not know what I was facing with my close association with Bill Perry and that I needed to get out and distance myself from Bill.

This was quite the soap opera that afternoon leading up to our show that night. Southern Thunder took the stage that night to the sound of a cheering crowd. It was a great show. This was fitting for what I was about to do. I finished the show with "An American Trilogy" by Elvis, and we received tears and a standing ovation from the audience. The band thought we were done. They were almost right. I waited for the crowd to quiet down and then told them that I wanted to do one more song: "Wind Beneath My Wings." I said, "I would like to dedicate this song to my band. They are a great band, and I will miss them. This is the last song I will be singing with Southern Thunder."

Talk about dropping a bombshell. The band was as shocked as the crowd. We played and sang our last song together with all we had. I sang through tears, and they played the same way as we realized that this was good-bye to something special that we all shared. We all gossiped about each other and with each other because that is what family does, and we were family. As the song ended, I could not escape fast enough, and I found out that I could not escape at all. The crowd was waiting to mob me, but the band got to me first. The guitarist and the bass player were hugging me and telling me that it didn't have to be like this. We could keep going. They did not understand what I had to do. I turned to Bob Williams, who was sitting in shock behind the drums. I pointed at him and told him to call Ty and for them to get after it. I made my way offstage and through the waiting crowd. I had one more stop to make. I had made my decision and was on a mission. I had to find me a long-haired drummer. I found him and told him that I was in. "Let me know when you need me to start, and I would be singing for Restless Heart now."

I got a ride to the airport and flew back to Dallas that night. My head and my emotions were still spinning from the events of the night, but I knew what I had to do. The next day I told Bill that I was done. I was leaving.

Bill got pretty upset with me. Actually, he got irate. He told me things about my parentage that did not sound very appropriate or even legal in this state. He told me that all the gifts that he had given me were not mine but belonged to the business. This even included a Jeep that I was driving at the time. I told him not to worry, I would see that it all got returned. I loaded all of it up in the Jeep and took off to Bill's house. I wanted Bill to know that I had stopped by. I decided that the best place to leave the Jeep and all the contents were right in the middle of the yard. It was very convenient for me. I drove right over the curb and right across his nice lawn, making sure that I left large ruts along my path of travel. I got out and walked away, leaving the keys, the Rolex watch, and anything else that would tie me to Bill Perry or Excelsior Music. I was free from him. As for Bill, shortly after all of this, he ended up as a guest of the fine state of Texas for thirty months, and I moved on.

It is sad when something that was so good ends like this. Bill and I ended up yelling at each other, but we had some great times together. I still have fond memories of our times together as a band. Bob Williams is no longer with us after he enjoyed a long career. Just a few years ago, I reconnected with Jim Lindsey, the steel guitar player. A friend of mine saw a video on YouTube that Jim had posted. It was our band playing "Too Cold to Hold." From that, I found Jim again. Jim had stayed with the band and played for Ty for twenty years. It turned out to be a good move for almost everybody. Ty Herndon's career took off, and some of the band stayed with him for years. From what I hear, Ty is now living very well in Southern California. I have not received a thank-you note from him. I think I deserve one for getting him some of his early gigs.

A short time after I left the band, I received a phone call from Todd Lohman, the owner of Caravan East in Albuquerque, New Mexico. It was a venue that I had played before. Southern Thunder was trying to get booked there. They had sent him an audition CD advertising Ty Herndon as the singer of Southern Thunder. There was only one problem. The audition was my songs and me singing. He played the CD for me over the phone. I shook my head in disbelief. Every year I find another part of this business that sinks to a new low. Is there ever a limit of how far a band manager will go to get a gig? Or how much someone will compromise their principles or flat out lie to get the results that they think they want? I didn't know whether to laugh at it, to be really pissed off, or to go shoot somebody.

I had already walked away, so I decided to just stay gone and keep pretty quiet about it. If somebody heard about it and asked me, I had plenty to say, but I did not bring up the issue myself. I do not blame Ty for any of this. Just as for me, a lot of things around him were not in his control. He was trying to get his break and was doing what he could to make it. Using my vocals to get gigs for the new band was not Ty's doing. I imagine like any artist he wanted to be known for his own talent, not piggybacking on mine. Ty went on to have a great career, and is truly a talent in his own right. If Ty happens to read this, I would love to hear it from his point of view. I would make a bet that he has his own stories to tell. It was also twenty years ago, and maturing has a way of changing your perspective.

I essentially walked off the plane and walked on the bus to tour with Restless Heart. Another great bunch of guys. We toured and wrote songs together. I was privileged to be a part of writing one of their biggest hits, "The Bluest Eyes in Texas." I seem to have an ability to weave Texas into a lot of my songs. What can I say? I love this state. It has given me some of my greatest adventures. The tour ends with Restless Heart, and we both decide to move on in our own paths.

I am now on my own again, and I have money in the bank. I am still in Texas and have time to decide what I want to do. I bounced around a little bit, looking for the next thing to spark my interest. I found myself in an interesting position. Many stories have a starving artist that is struggling to make it every step of the way. I have been in this position before and since this, but right now I was still comfortable and could afford to wait for what was coming next. As I was telling my story, I was thinking back to where my money was coming from. I had money coming in from HT and other places. I found out that there was money being given to me every month. It was coming from an undisclosed source. I later found out that it was coming from Elvis through the name of a family trust of a distant relative.

In the course of my travels around the area, I ran into some people that were associated with a private academy that provided for displaced and orphaned children. For obvious reasons, this is a topic that is dear to my heart. The name of this academy was Happy Hill Farms. A gentleman named Ed Shipman was the president. As is often the case, within a day or two, I was making direct contact with Ed. We found things in common right away, and I began to look for ways that I could use my talents to benefit Happy Hills. Ed Shipman had ties to the Dallas Cowboys, and before I knew it, I was performing at events that were being hosted by the Cowboys organization. This led to some more great experiences, and I sang at a couple of notable events. One of them was for the Dallas Cowboys charity banquet, where Happy Hills was the beneficiary, and another was the NFL Alumni banquet. It was at a time when prayer was not allowed at these gatherings as a result of a push to not exclude other religions by promoting Christianity. You can call it what you want. I exercise my faith and never demand that others join in. I don't look down on people that believe differently than I do, but I don't think that they should have the right to tell me what I can't do.

I was asked to sing the Lord's Prayer at the banquet. It was deemed to be acceptable because I was singing it, not praying it. I still had to have an attorney and a union representative both present to make sure that nothing discriminatory was taking place. It seems to me that common sense is becoming less and less common. After I sang the Lord's Prayer, I thanked the crowd and was walking back to my seat when the emcee walked up to the microphone. He looked down to where Troy Aikman and Jay Novacek, two of the star Cowboys players, were sitting. Earlier that year, both of them had tried their hands at music and had released songs. He said, "Troy and Jay, the next time the two of you think of doing something stupid, like singing another song, remember this, because what you just heard, that was singing!"

I feel like my days in Texas are wrapping up for a while. This is not everything that happened to me in Texas. I will need several more books to tell all the stories. There will be more to come. There are still some good ones to tell. For now, I make plans for a short trip back to Louisiana before I go visit my oldest sister in Phoenix. Little do I know that the trip to Phoenix will change my whole life.

Marie and Me

I was not there to know what the relationship was like between Elvis and my mom. I will let her tell it from her perspective in her time. There are some things that I do know. I know that Elvis cared enough about my mom to stay in contact with her. There are pictures of Elvis, Priscilla, my mom, and Glen Campbell all together. This picture was taken at George Klein's wedding in December of 1970. The wedding was held in the private suite belonging to Elvis in Las Vegas. Elvis was best man at the wedding. When this picture was taken, I would have been nine years old. All of this tells me that Elvis maintained a friendship with my mom over the years. I don't know how long it lasted, but it lasted.

There are cashier's checks that Elvis sent to my mom to provide for her well-being. When my mom traveled to Vegas or Hawaii, she stayed in places reserved for Elvis. One of the biggest indicators of how Elvis felt about his time with my mom was shown when Elvis commissioned the writing of a song that just missed becoming his seventeenth number-one hit. The song became popular in the later part of 1961—the year that I was born. The song was "(Marie's the Name) His Latest Flame."

I will let my mom fill in her details. This is how I came to know Zona Marie, the woman I call Mother.

From the time that I can remember being able to remember, I saw my mom from time to time. I didn't know that this kind lady that I saw from time to time really was my mom. I was under the impression that she was an old friend of the family who really seemed to like us kids. I always knew that I had been adopted. The adoption of my sisters and I had been explained to me as a family solution to a hard situation that my mom was facing. Before my birth, my mom was in the process of finalizing a divorce from a womanizing man. This man had been out fathering other children at the same time that my mom was having his children. She was facing the mountainous task of not only surviving on her own, but doing so with three small children. Her ex was busy with all his other children and would not be providing any help or support for my mom or my sisters. The solution was arrived at with the Smith family stepping in. I believe this happened in part because this is what a Christian family does in the South, and also because of who my father was, and that family wanted to keep me close by.

I had a happy childhood. I did not want for anything. I was basically raised by grandparents. They had a pretty good handle on life and were very secure. The lady that I later learned was my mom used to come visit at the house when she could. At one point, she only lived two blocks away. It was all explained to me in a very grown-up way. I have had several people ask me about the trauma of growing up as an adopted child or about feeling rejected by my birth mom. I did not feel any of that. I don't ever remember lying awake at night wondering why my mom didn't love me. In fact, it was the opposite. I felt more cared for because I had a good, stable, loving home to grow up in. Years later, when the pieces started to fall into place, I realized that I had a sincere and loving mom who would visit when she could. Understand this about me. I am not masking over deep-seated pain in my psyche. I am not hiding from my feelings here. I look at life fairly simply. And very practically. My situation is all I knew. I am also explaining my life from the child's perspective that I was experiencing at the time. I do not pretend to understand or even try to identify what it was like for my mom when, at the end of her visits with us, she had to say good-bye every time and to not tuck us in or have breakfast in the morning with her children. That is her story, and I will let her tell it in her own words.

I always felt nothing but love and caring from her when I saw her. Children innately know when adults are being authentic and when they are putting on an act. I knew my mom was a good and genuine person, and that is all I needed to know. Once I knew that about her, everything was good. I could get back to the important business of my life, which for me meant playing. In that regard, not much has changed to this very day. It was a good life. I had everything I needed. I accepted the facts about my life and kept going. I have lived my adult life looking forward to the next event or adventure while still enjoying the present moments. I don't remember feeling any differently as a child. I suspect that my memories of a happy and fun childhood are because I was happy, and it was fun. I have plenty of emotion in my life, and this was not a time that fostered negative ones. I had a good childhood, especially by today's standards. It may be hard to fathom, but I did not feel like I was missing out on anything as a child. As I grew into a man, I found out that while I did not feel slighted in my growing up, there was now something that I wanted. And what I wanted was to know my mom and to have her in my life. There were two distinct events that brought out this feeling in me.

One was becoming a parent when I was in my early twenties. I learned what it means to have a child looking to you for direction and protection. For a fun-loving and free-living young artist, this was a sobering idea. To have a young life depending on you for their well-being and even their life changes your outlook on life. It also gave me a new perspective on my mom's situation—what she was facing and how heartbreaking the hard decisions were that were facing her. I wonder how many people around her were pressuring her to make a practical decision without being able to understand how a mother's heart was being ripped out of her chest by the decisions that she was making to save her children. It's an understatement to say that when I had a child and then, four years later, had to leave my own child behind because of a divorce, my perspective on my own upbringing dramatically changed.

I had started working for MCI. I was installing calling card table-top phones. MCI was having them installed in truck stops so truckers could talk to their families at home over the dinner table, something to lessen the feeling of separation that truckers experience in the long days away from home.

I had the Southern route, which included Texas and Louisiana. When I found out that I was heading back to Louisiana, something clicked. I needed to talk to my mom.

I had made my way back to Louisiana and was near to where I grew up. I made a phone call to Buddy. Buddy had my mom's phone number. I need to back up a little bit. Growing up, I thought that Buddy was my dad. My mom was in the process of divorcing him when she was pregnant with me. Buddy made a good cover story. ID and Etta suggested that he may have been my real dad, and I never had a cause to question it until years later. One more twist in the saga of a Southern family was this. As I have already stated, ID was Gladys Presley's brother. ID was married to Etta. Etta's maiden name was Roach. Buddy's last name was Roach. It is a long branch of the family tree, but I was related by marriage to both of my adopted parents. Welcome to the South.

Buddy and I were always cordial. After getting to know him and his ways, I was even more glad that I had the adopted parents that I had. I never asked him why, if he was my supposed father, did he give me up? I didn't care. If it had been true that Buddy was my biological father, I was grateful that he did give me up for adoption. He was not the type of man that I wanted to come from or to learn about life and living from. I did not want to be like him.

After getting my mom's phone number, I was still nervous. I was also determined, so I called the number that I got from Buddy. My mom answered the phone. At the sound of her voice, a flood of emotion and memories came over me. I heard the same thing in her voice. I tried to keep it in check as we talked and set a date to meet for lunch at Pat's Seafood in Saint Charles, Louisiana. I still have a hard time with my emotions, at least displaying them in public. I have been onstage so much and am expected to be the entertainment, so I present an image.

An image that is fun and happy-go-lucky, without a care in the world. It has become something that I hide behind. Part of the reason is that I have learned that if people know that they can hurt you, they will try. I am not cynical; it is just a fact in my business. I also like to be in control of my environment. When my emotions break through to the surface, I definitely feel out of control. This short conversation with my mom is letting me know that I am on emotional thin ice. It won't take much to break through. I can feel it coming, and I haven't even seen her face-to-face yet. At least not in many years. The next time I see her will be the first time I call her Mother.

A thought had crossed my mind. I wonder what it was like for her to be in our house and to hear the word *Mom* and have to stifle her response to that word? Did she have to keep reminding herself that I was talking to or talking about Etta? This was probably a question that I would not ask. There was enough pain in her past. I did not need to bring up anything more.

I find myself a few days later sitting in my truck outside of Pat's. I am early and nervous, two things I rarely am. After waiting as long as I can and still not seeing my mom come by, I decide to go in and wait. She is only a few minutes late, and I am working up a nasty Louisiana sweat out in the humidity. I ask for a table for two, and while I am being walked to my booth, I look down, and I make eye contact with my mom in another booth. I stop dead in my tracks, startled and staring. My mom was nervous and excited too. She showed up an hour early because she could not stand to pace in circles in her house any longer while waiting for the hands on the clock to move. I am not sure at what point the hostess walks away as I am trying to come up with the right words. My mom breaks the silence by calling my name. I will never understand what it is, but no matter how old you are, there is something about the loving voice of a mother calling your name that has a deep effect on a child. Remember that emotion that I was trying to keep in check? So much for that idea. I am not sure how we should greet each other, so I slide quickly into my side of the booth, and for a moment we clasp hands across the table as we look at each other. Sons usually do not think of their mothers as being strikingly beautiful, but my mom is. She has carried herself and her years well.

After a few moments that lasted forever, we start the conversation awkwardly. And then another awkward moment. The waitress asks us what we would like to drink. I could really use a drink. There are times that I want a drink. Right now, I need a drink. I am hesitant to order one. Drinking was not encouraged in my growing up, and I am not sure what my mom's opinion is on the subject. She was thinking the same thing. She looks at me and says, "I could really use a drink."

I grin and nod. "Me too." This breaks the ice. We have a common starting point. The conversation now begins. It is odd in a way to see this woman that I have known sparingly as I grew up. It is strange to make the transition from family friend to mom. It is strange, but the transition is happening. At least I have a head start. I know something about her. This is not like getting to know a complete stranger.

Within a few minutes, it becomes obvious to me that this is one of those lunches that is going to last well past dinnertime. Those emotions that I was so worried about holding so tightly are finding a comfortable place that

I can be myself and relax. It is an intensely emotional conversation but a safe one. I put enough money on the edge of our table to cover our meal three times over, hoping they get the message that I do not want to be bothered or asked if we are ready to leave. We are playing the most wonderful game of catch-up. It starts out with what we have in common. The visits we shared growing up. The times she and her friends came to see me perform. How she felt as a mom watching me grow and perform on stage. Part of her swelling up with pride as she saw me doing so well. Part of her hurting inside as she saw the reminder of my father in me. At times feeling like her heart was being crushed by not being free to reach out and draw me to her in the way a mother is meant to embrace her child. The grand story of life that is filled with joy and pain, sadness and elation, pride and sorrow. All of what makes us who we are. I am reliving it with her.

For myself, I am in the presence of love. Real motherly love for the first time, free and unencumbered. We are still getting to know each other gradually and cautiously. We are looking for signs of hurt or emotional damage in each other. We don't want to tread carelessly on each other's feelings. Through it all, I feel one thing from her. I feel the love that my mom has for me. ID had a son from a previous marriage, so he knew what it is to be a dad. Etta did her best, but she never had any biological children of her own. You can't give away what you don't have, and so Etta could never give me a mother's love, no matter how hard she tried. This may explain why ID and my mom always seemed to get along so well and why Etta was more withdrawn. Etta may have been worried that she could never have what my mom has with me and was troubled that I might notice this difference and gravitate to my mom over her. I had grown up never feeling unloved, but now I was in the presence of something different. I don't know how to describe it, except to say that it felt right. We had things to discuss and to work out, but we were heading in the same direction together, and we would get there. I get an idea of what Kenny Rogers had said to me years before. "You can't write about it unless you have lived it." Now this makes sense. I had written about moms before, but I didn't realize how deep that love and connection is. Until now.

As the hours flew by, we continued to catch up on the details of our lives, like what we had been doing in the previous years that the other one didn't yet know about. She loved my stories of Lawrence Welk and other experiences. She did not in any way seem surprised at my talent or success. I never thought to ask her where my talent may have come from. As we began to wind down our time together, she let me know where I got my talent from. She told me that everyone agreed to let me believe that Buddy was my father, but in fact I came from somewhere else. It made sense to me as I had wondered if I had a real mom and a real dad, why wasn't I living with one of them. By the time I started to wonder about this, ID and Etta had both passed away, so there were no answers. Until now.

My mom seemed to be nervous again, a look I had not seen for the last few hours. She leaned across the table toward me. Not to keep our conversation private. It was past closing time at Pat's, and we were the only ones left. She seemed to be trying to lessen the distance between us so that I could feel the importance and the emotion in what she was about to tell me. I could tell that we were at another important point in our conversation. She looked me in the eyes and slowly and carefully told me the story of Elvis being my father. This was a lot to take in. I am not sure why, but I did not give this revelation a whole lot of importance at the time. Maybe my emotions could not process this new information completely. Maybe I was feeling like this was not as important as the woman sitting across the table from me. That is what my heart was feeling. I couldn't quite control my brain at the time. What should have been earth-shattering news to me, a great revelation, was almost a side note in my head. My mom seemed to be relieved that I did not ask too many questions or details about my parentage. I was more interested in recent history, the kind that I remember.

The details of that relationship are also not the details that a mother shares with her son. Our conversation was coming to an end, and we both had a lot to process. We finally walked out of the restaurant and parted with a kiss and a hug and a promise to keep in touch with each other. I am not sure what happened after that. I am not sure why I did not contact my mom for a while. I had a lot of information and emotions to process. The information was easy. I and emotions take a while. By the time I was ready to call her again, I had become busy with other ventures, and I also could not find her number again. Buddy had passed away, and I was not going to call him again anyway.

The other thing that changed my life with regard to my mother occurred one day when I opened a drawer and opened what I thought was a closed chapter in my life. I was visiting my sister Emma in Phoenix. One morning

Emma had left for work, and I was rummaging around the kitchen, looking for something. I pulled open the junk drawer by the phone and saw a corner of an envelope. That corner had my mom's name on it. This caught my eye and my breath as I recognized the writing as my mom's. I reached for the envelope and saw that it was addressed to me. In the years since I had grown, it had been explained to me who my mom really was. When my adopted parents had passed away, I felt that is was okay to start asking questions about my real mom. I learned that the lady that came to visit was in fact my birth mom. I had some cards that she had given me when I was a child. I had gone back and read them over and over to try and get a clue to how my mom felt about her only son. From this I had come to recognize her writing.

Curious and anxious, I reached for the card and found that it was the first envelope in a whole stack. I was curious and hesitant at the same time. Hidden letters rarely bring good news. And why were my letters hidden at my sister's house? And if Emma could look me in the eye and talk about mom and never mention this, what else is there? "What else is there?" felt like it was starting to become the theme of my life. Most people find out more about their lives as they grow up. With every new thing I found, it seemed to reveal that there was more that I did not know. In some aspects of my life, it felt like I was living life in emotional reverse.

Staring at the envelopes and trying to soak in the possibilities of what it could mean and why they were with Emma, I decided that they were mine to open. They had my name on them. I was concerned, but not too apprehensive. More curious than scared of the contents, for two reasons: They were from my mom, and until now, I knew that my mom had expressed love for me. They were also the kind of envelopes that cards come in. I was right. Each one of them were birthday cards, one for every birthday of my life growing up. She never missed one of them. That answers the question about whether or not I was on her mind or if she ever thought of me.

Later that day, I asked Emma about them, and I got an awkward silence. I hate awkward silences. They are always followed by a response that is usually meant to protect the interests of the one being silent. They almost never are looking out for my best interests. Emma explained to me that she got them from Etta, our adopted mom. Etta was, it turns out, a bit jealous over my mom. I think she was also jealous about how well my mom got along with ID. Etta kept the cards from me in part because of how she felt about my mom, and I believe in part because I always seemed to be the special one, and she didn't want my sisters to feel left out and not cared for. My sisters had a no-account deadbeat for a dad, and even though we didn't know our dads, mine was a rock star, and that might make a difference. People say that kids are funny. Well, guess what? Grown-ups are pretty funny too.

Seeing that stack of birthday cards struck a chord and woke something up in me, a feeling that was new to me. I had been without my adopted mom since she had passed several years before, and for the first time, something was missing. I missed my mom. It wasn't that I missed having a mom in my life. It was that I missed my mom. I wanted to find her again and find out who she was and have my mom in my life. From everything that I had been told and from what I read in these cards, she believed in me and loved me, and I wanted to know this woman. I was encouraged to go find her, but I did not have her number. The only thing I had was the address labeled on the envelopes. She did not live there anymore.

I was going to have to get creative. Lucky for me, I am creative. I knew the area she was in last time, and I started there. I struck out several times before I found a town with several people with her last name. I was not having any luck with any of these numbers and thought I was at a dead end. I had a thought to call the local police station in the hopes that a small-town police department might know the citizens of the town. I didn't think about how it would sound later. That in trying to reach my mom, I thought the police might know who she was. That they might have a file on her. This was not my reasoning. I didn't have a good reason. I just had a feeling. I was thinking that the police department in a small town might know everyone's business, and maybe someone might have heard of my mom.

I called and talked to an efficient but friendly lady at the small-town station where I hoped my mom was living. I explained to her what I was trying to do. I told her about being adopted and seeing my mom before and trying to find her again. How the people that we had in common had passed away, and I was having difficulty locating her. Did anyone there at the station know my mom or her family? The lady informed me that she could not give out any information about anyone in the town, and yet there was something in this woman's voice that told me she knew something—something that she didn't feel like she was free to share with me. I could tell that my story had touched her mother's heart. I asked her if

I could leave her my name and number so that if anyone did know my mom or if someone heard of her, they could give her my number, and she could call me. The nice lady seemed relieved that she had an out. She had a way to help me without giving away any information. I thanked her for her time and to please remember me.

Ten minutes later, my phone rings. It is the lady from the police station again. In an abrupt voice, she gives me a name and a phone number. She tells me that this may work and wishes me the best of luck. I am left startled and staring at this number. Here it is. I know it in my gut that this is my mom's house. I still have the same strange sense of urgency to find her again. After a few moments of gazing at the phone number and collecting my thoughts, I dial the phone.

I need to let you know what was going on with my mom at this time. For some time, she had been feeling like she needed to share her heart with me. To tell me all about her life, my life, and whatever else was on her heart. After pondering it for a while, she finally wrote that letter to me. She was still unsure and carried it with her for some time. One day she showed it to her mom and asked her mom what she should do with it. Her mom read it and, without hesitation, told her to mail it. It stayed in her purse for a few more days. Soon after her mom told her to mail it, my mom left the house for a physical therapy appointment and decided that this was the day to mail me the letter. The post office was close to her appointment, and she was all out of reasons not to send it. After her appointment, she dropped it in the mailbox and prayed all the way home that it would find me and that I would find her.

This was what was going on while I was trying to track my mom down. I dialed the number. A man answered the phone, and I identified myself. I told him what I was trying to do. He said, "Hello, Dennis. I am your mother's husband. You can call me Pappy."

My heart jumped. I found her. Pappy went on to tell me that at that very moment, my mom was at the post office mailing me a letter. He would be sure to have her call me, and he was so looking forward to meeting me. I could not believe it. My mom and I were both searching for the same thing at the same time. I could not get to Louisiana fast enough to see her again.

When my mom walked in the door, still praying about her letter that she just sent, Pappy handed her a note and told her to call this number and talk to her son. Her son was waiting to hear from her. She says that she almost passed out. She believes that God answers prayers, but this was ridiculous.

Shortly after that, my mom came to visit me, and ever since that day, there is not a week that goes by that we do not talk. We will never lose each other again.

Elvis Lives On

Elvis is my daddy, but who are all these people, and what do they want with me?

I don't know of anyone that was so large in life and has become so much larger than life since he has been gone. By the time I was starting to make my own moves in my life, his life was ending. For me and for millions of fans worldwide, the death of Elvis was just the beginning. I wonder if he was aware of what was going on in my life at this time? In some regard, I am fortunate that Elvis was such a superstar. Because of who he was, I have the opportunity that I never would have if my dad had just been an ordinary man. If this had been the case, I might have had a scrapbook and a photo album to commemorate who my father was and little else to go with it.

Because Elvis was Elvis, so many details of his life are available to me. His every move is detailed, and I have so many moments of him on film and tape. I am grateful for all the access I have to him and the time that I get to spend with him. I spend a lot of time just him and me. When I am listening to his recording sessions or singing along with him, the years between us disappear, and I feel like we are connected. I have had the opportunity to sing some of his songs using his studio tracks, so I am singing to the same music that he did.

Elvis also left me another gift: the association of people that were close to him. From my adopted dad, to my manager (HT), to Elvis's good friend Sherrill Nielsen, and the Jordanaires. These men were directly and indirectly influential in my raising and in my career. These men all showed me about living. That living is a journey. It is not the mad rush that was the ruin of my father. It is a steady journey, with ups and downs. Whichever one you are currently experiencing, whether a high or a low, something else is coming. They told me to not forget who you are in the highs and to be careful not to lose yourself in the lows. Either one of these mistakes can keep you from ever reaching your potential. I do admit that in some areas, I am a slow learner, and some of these lessons have taken a few of the cycles of life to sink in. I am grateful that I am still here and still have the ability to keep going. It is never too late to learn. I am thankful to have been spared many of the pitfalls that ended the careers of my contemporaries. At the same time, I wish I might have learned more of what made others around me more successful. Whatever may have happened or didn't happen, I am here now. Now, at this time. I am ready for the next of several chapters in my life. I eagerly look forward to what is coming. I am fully prepared to enjoy it, as I now have the ability to appreciate every day of it.

Exploring the Elvis Connections

Many people have a story to tell about a time when they saw Elvis or met him one time. I have a different story. I never really remember spending time with him. I was onstage with Elvis and Sherrill Nielsen at least once, but I was a kid and was always sharing the stage with grown-ups. It must be hard to imagine not being more cognizant of what was going on around me. Performing around people that were famous was the norm for me. This was normal. I was a kid, and I didn't know that I was supposed to be awestruck. I have pictures of Elvis holding me and of me hanging out of his tour bus window. All of these can be explained as coincidences. What cannot be explained away as coincidence is all the documents and personal effects that I have received over the years. You also cannot explain away family and all the people who worked with Elvis and showed up in my life and never left. Time has begun to take some of these people from us. We lost Sherrill Neilsen last year. This is one of the other reasons for this book. I want to tell my story and tell about the investment in my life that some very good people made while they are still here to appreciate it. One last thing that you cannot explain away is that Elvis and I, we share the same DNA. I have known in my heart that Elvis is my daddy for years. It has been a part of my life for years. I know it. I feel it. There are too many of what other people call coincidences in my life. I don't call them coincidence. I call them part of my life and my heritage. I have been getting compared to Elvis for years. Ever since I was a kid.

One day when I was at the *Lawrence Welk Show*, a reporter came to write a story about Lawrence and the show. I was brought in as one of the young new singers that was a part of the show. I was singing an Elvis song for Lawrence, and here is what the reporter wrote.

> Dennis Smith joins the group. Dennis, 17, connected with the show when it was visiting his home town in Louisiana. He'd taken two elderly aunts to see Lawrence and at the end of the evening, when the audience was invited up on stage to dance, Dennis asked if he could sing instead, since he didn't dance too well. After he had finished his number, someone shouted, "Why don't you hire him?" and Lawrence replied, "We will."
>
> Would I also like to hear Dennis sing? Dennis smiles an aw-shucks grin and sets into "Love Me Tender" a cappella. Lawrence again turns, beams his approval, and suggests Dennis try it once again, "but clean it up a little."
>
> Without a pause, Dennis tears into a cleaner version of the song. Good, good, but Lawrence suggests it one more time, half a tone higher. Without a flicker of protest, his grin suitably fastened, Dennis is again out-Presleying Presley. (Zukowski, Helen. 1979. *Palm Springs Life*.)

Shaun "Sherrill" Nielsen

Elvis said that Sherrill was his favorite singer. They had a special relationship and mutual respect for each other. Theirs was a friendship that began before I was born. Sherrill was with Elvis when he came to see me and my mom at the hospital at my birth. I still have the blanket that Elvis brought to me at the hospital. I obviously do not remember this taking place. I do understand what it means. It is one more event that shows me that I may not have been expected, but my mom and I were important and cared for. I don't have any evidence that Elvis was there at the hospital. What I do have is important to me. It may be dismissed as circumstantial to other people. It is pretty solid to me. I have the blanket that I mentioned. I have something more though. I have the word of a man that befriended me ever since I knew him. A man that brought me a warm fleece blanket for my bed because he was concerned that my little apartment in Nashville was not warm enough in the winter. A man that asked me if I was in need of anything whenever he saw me. A man that was eager to have me try on the fur coat that Elvis had given him. He wanted to see how it looked on me. He tried to give it to me. I could not take it. it swallowed me up; it was so big. I couldn't take it because it was a gift from his friend and hero. I have in my life a man that, while he lay dying, took off the necklace that Elvis had given to him, and he tried to give that to me. I could not accept that either. It was a symbol of a deep and lasting friendship. I wanted Sherrill to have it with him for it to be a comfort to him in his last moments. I have the friendship and caring of this good man. I have the word of Sherrill Nielsen that he was there to see some of my first moments of life. Right by the side of his best friend, my dad. In a business that will lie, cheat, and steal from you, I have the word of a man that has never lied to me. A man that always wanted the best for me and saw the best in me.

I have the word of another also. The word of my mother. Moms may do anything to protect their children, and my mom would do that for me. She has nothing to gain. It would have been easier for me and offered the guarantee of a normal uneventful life had my mom told the story that I was fathered by her philandering ex-husband. That would have been simple and believable. My mom has had many opportunities to lie to me, and she doesn't. We have an understanding about that. She knows the things that were kept from me while I was a child and a young man. We don't keep anything from each other. I have the word of a woman that will not lie about an event that is very dear to her—the birth of her only son. A son by a man whom she loved and who loved her, in the way he knew how or was allowed to show.

I have another noteworthy event about my birth. In the summer of 2012, I met an Episcopal priest. He was told to come see me play at a gig in Phoenix. It was just me and a guitar and a crowd in a bar. After I came offstage, Father James introduced himself to me and asked if he could speak with me for a few moments. A mutual friend had heard of his story and told the priest that he needed to come see me perform and then make up his own mind. This may seem odd to you, but I can't count the number of strange-sounding introductions that come my way. It has become commonplace for me. It runs the gamut from people that know people that I know to people that I have never met, but they walk in and ask me how my mom is, and they call her by name. It is uncanny and happens all the time. I just go with it anyway.

Father James asks and tells me in the same sentence. "You are somebody?"

"Yes, I am. I am John."

"No. I mean you are somebody! You have a history!"

Okay. This is getting a little stranger than normal, but he is a priest after all. He doesn't seem strange.

"Yes, I do have a history. I have lived quite a life."

"No. I mean about where you come from. About your dad!"

"I know who my dad is. Why don't you tell me what you think?"

"My friend knows my story and told me to come see you, and then I would know if you are the one."

Oh boy! I hope he's not leaving reality here. I really hope the good father is not going to tell me that I am the chosen one or that I am the Messiah. Where is he going with this?

I give a long-drawn-out "Ohhh-kay?" as I glance around to see if there are any monks in hooded robes milling about.

The good father takes a breath and gets his excitement under control. Maybe he realizes how strange this is sounding. After all, I do not know what he knows.

"Let me back up a little bit. I have some pictures from my grandmother. I have had them for years, and I think she entrusted them to me because of my priesthood."

"Yes?" I still don't see the connection.

I have had these pictures for years, and even though my grandmother took the pictures with her camera and gave them to me, I don't feel that they belong to me."

"Okay. Who do you think they belong to?"

"Our mutual friend told me that after I saw you that I would know."

By now we are both leaning forward across the table. The intensity of his voice and the seriousness of his eyes match the tone of his voice. I am locked in now. He has my attention.

"This keeps coming up. That you will know. What will you know?"

"I will know that I have something that belongs to you."

"Let me get this straight because this is the oddest conversation that I have had this week. You are visiting from halfway across the country, and we have never met, and yet you have something that belongs to me. It is from your dead grandmother that I don't even know. What could you possibly have of mine?"

"Let me tell you a little bit about my grandmother first. When she was a younger lady, she worked as a labor and delivery nurse in a small hospital in a small town in Texas."

Okay. Now the hair on the back of my neck is rising up as I am waiting for the other baby booty to drop. I don't even notice that I have stopped breathing.

"One day my grandmother was taking care of a new baby boy who was born to a sweet young mother. While my grandmother was there, the father came in, accompanied by a friend of his. He was so happy and tender with mother and child. He brought a baby blanket for his new son. My grandmother recognized the father and asked if they would like some pictures taken. She took those pictures of mother, father, and child. She never had the chance to give the pictures to them. She always held on to them and often wondered what became of that baby boy. She expected to hear news of him, but never did."

"And where do I fit into this story?" I already suspect that I know the answer, but I want to hear the rest of the story from him. I want to know if he is as sane as I hope he is. If he really has what he claims to, it is one more piece of my history that again is falling strangely into my lap.

There is a catch in his voice as he prepares to answer the reason that he is here to see me and at the thought that he has found what he has been looking for.

"Helen told me that if I saw you that I would know if Elvis is your father, and that I have pictures of you as a baby with your mom and dad."

"So? What do you think?"

"I don't think! I know! I have what belongs to you, John Smith!"

I never know where this stuff is coming from. I do not go looking. It finds me. Father James and I had a great conversation afterward, and he left with my contact information. This was the last I heard from him. I am left wondering about where he is and what he is doing. I would love to have those pictures. It would be one more page of the scrapbook of my interesting life. I don't need it to know who I am, but I would love to have them. I would also like to thank Father James again for holding on to a piece of my life so faithfully for so long.

Do I call this encounter proof of who I am? Not at all. I am not searching for proof. I know who I am. This story is a bit incredible, and I am hesitant to share it because I know how it sounds, especially against the backdrop of all the other stories about the other "children of Elvis." Stories that range from the real Lisa Marie being whisked away at birth and raised in Switzerland, to a son of Elvis being adopted by circus performers to hide the fact that his dancer mom from Vegas had a relationship with Elvis. Even Lucky Rocket, a young man who is still in hiding in Hollywood while he prepares to make a movie and release an album that will announce to the world that he is the son of the king. There are some interesting stories, to say the least. I share my story because I sat across the table from this man who had nothing to gain. I saw the look in his eyes and listened to his voice. I am convinced that he believes the story to be true. He and I both believe the same story, and he knows things that only somebody that had direct knowledge of the events would know. Can I prove it to you? No. I don't feel like I need to. I am just telling you my story about my life. I believe it. Through these pages, I hope you get to know me and understand me a little better. I know what I know, and what you decide is up to you.

HT or Harrison Tyner

Harrison Tyner. The first time I heard of him was after a fishing trip that ID had taken on Sam Rayburn Lake in Texas. ID was talking to a friend of his about how to get something going in Nashville for me. His friend told him to call Don Fowler. Don had a record label in Nashville, and they all knew Don. They weren't sure what all Don could do for me, but Don had a partner named HT. HT could take care of whatever Don could not do. Besides, ID and HT had some good musical friends in common from their musician days on the road. HT seemed more than eager to talk to ID about me. He told my adopted dad that he wanted to manage my singing career for as long as I wanted, and he sealed the deal with a handshake. ID asked HT if they needed a contract. HT told him that he could have a contract if he wanted one, but they had just shook hands, and that was good enough for him. Apparently, it was good enough for ID too.

The first time I met HT, he was visiting us at our home in Louisiana. I was not in on most of the discussions. My recollection is that they were planning a strategy for my career path. I am not sure when the conversation happened, but at some point HT had a discussion that he was there because of a promise he made to my father: a promise to watch me and to watch out for me. Over the years, HT has been a constant in my life. He has been a mixture of manager, producer, mentor, confidant, friend, and guide. HT was in a group called the Landsman while he was attending Pepperdine University in Malibu, California. Music has been a part of his life ever since then.

"Young man. Do you want to be rich, or do you want to be famous?" This was the voice of HT on the other end of the phone, one of the many questions that he has posed to me during our years together. At times I was unsure if I was supposed to be learning something from his questions or if he was just messing with my head. Lord knows I did enough things to mess with his head and very well his mental health during his tenure with me. HT has played an interesting role in my life. He has never forced or pushed me into anything. He has supported and guided me as I have shown interests in different projects and ideas. He was billed as my manager, but he never took the control of my life that most managers do. It seemed to me that he was content to let me be until I decided I was ready for another go-round in the music business. I have many interests in life, and over the years many different endeavors have caught my interest. Because of this and because of some of the fickleness of the music business, I have taken breaks over the years. Every time I came back to music, HT was there.

I have had an interesting relationship with HT over the years. Looking back, I have some questions about his promise to my father and how that promise affected my career and career choices. HT will only answer some questions about me and what was going on behind the scenes. At times he says as much with his silence as he does with his words. There are some topics in my life that he remains silent about. It is my observation that sometimes people say as much with what they say as with what they do not say.

I can only guess on some areas that concern my life. I can only guess that the people that were watching me and watching out for me were mostly concerned that I had the chances that my father did not have. That I would have the opportunity to have a life of my choosing. That I would not get caught up in the grinding wheel of fame and fortune that will use you and then crush you under the weight of the image that was created to promote you. That I would not follow in all of the footsteps of Elvis. They had seen the dark side of success and wanted to protect me from this. I had the benefit of growing up with a certain amount of success but was not ever on the cover of magazines, except for the local phone book, or all over the news. I wonder about this also. Was there a limit to how much success I was allowed to obtain, or was it all my own doing? Was Elvis ever concerned that if I began to gather more recognition, my talent might have been recognized? If this happened, would the public have started to ask questions about our similarities? Was this something that everyone was trying to avoid? To keep both Elvis and me from having to answer questions that would affect our fans and our futures? Given my penchant for going off in different directions, was there a caution that I may not follow the prescribed path they hoped that I would take?

At times there are more questions than answers about my life. One thing that I can't question is the intent of those that Elvis trusted to watch me. Like all parents do, they may make mistakes, but I have to respect their motivation. I don't believe that anyone ever set out to harm me or keep me from my ultimate destiny. I believe that they were honorable men keeping a promise to a man that they all honored. They honored him and their vow by caring for me. Always with the best of intentions from their point of view. It must have been difficult to have been put in this position, the position of acting as a surrogate parent and guide to me. To accept the responsibility of making sure that I followed the right path when they were helpless to protect my father from his own undoing. To watch Elvis start out so strong and then face so many struggles, while his friends could only watch and hope. Did they go to extremes at times to protect me too much? Were they ever watchful of any indication that I might end up in the same condition as my father? Again, a lot of questions. Again, I am grateful to all of them, and I am grateful for my life. I am grateful to Elvis for caring enough to have the ones that he trusted watch out for me.

My attorney is a good man named Jim Carroll. He has become a friend as well as an advisor and counselor. I asked him how to answer the big question about who my father is. He says to tell the truth. I believe that Elvis is my father. I do not have personal knowledge of this fact as I was quite young when it occurred. I have a bucketload of information, personal effects, and the testimony of people that were there. I share family and family traits with my father. I have the word of people that I trust. I have a lot of evidence. Not to be contrary, but how do you know who your dad is? Do you remember being conceived? I submit to you that my story of determining who my father is isn't that much different than your story. Mine just has some extra details as it involved a secret birth, an adoption, a cover-up, and the king of rock and roll.

My buddy Rich and I were musing one day that if my daddy was the king of rock and roll and my brother-in-law was the prince of pop, what does that make me? I submit to you that you cannot personally testify as to who your parents are. You are told by those that you trust and love. There are documents that provide evidence. Some of the personality traits and physical similarities may be passed down to you. You may have some of the same quirks. All of these things add up to a certain amount of evidence that convinces you that your parents belong to you. I have all of these things. The only element that appears to make my story harder to believe is that one of the parents involved in my story is a celebrity. I realize that this is a big sticking point. Because of the history of other people that have made fraudulent claims, it can make my story harder to believe. It is kind of a catch-22 for me.

When I tell my story to people, I find that the majority of the people have one of two different responses. There is one group that believes me because they believe that it is true. They don't need to see any documentation. The other response is that they believe me after they have seen the documentation that I have to offer. There is a small portion that is left. Those few will not believe anything no matter what they hear or see. If Elvis himself were to be resurrected and appear to them and identify me as his son, I still think that they would be skeptical.

We have had a lot of long discussions on how to handle this and what approach we should take with this book. There have been as many ideas as there have been people that we have talked to. From a tell-all, revealing personal secrets and indiscretions of the characters, to promoting theories that Elvis is still alive. We were told that we have to make it juicy and salacious to gain a bigger audience, to let the reader hear about the behind-the-scenes secrets.

If you want to read about all of that, then there are plenty of books out there for you. I am writing this book and telling my story for a different reason. I wanted to write down my story because it is my story, and it is true. I have heard rumors and stories that others claim to be true. Those stories are not in here. I am only putting down what I personally know to be true by firsthand accounts. I am not writing this to convince the unbelieving. Skeptics I can understand, and I appreciate their position. I have questioned it myself at times. I can't do anything about the unbelievers.

I decided that I wanted to include pictures and documentation in this book. I felt the need to do this for several reasons. It is an incredible story. If it were to be told to me, I would want to see some backup documentation. The story has been told before by people without any documentation to back it up. One man owns an Elvis museum, and he went to court to have his name legally changed, but I don't see that he has any documentation to tie him to the family, much less to Elvis. I believe that the fans of Elvis deserve something more than that.

The biggest reason for all of this is that the story of my life is important to me, and so are the people that are a part of it. As I said before, I am not doing all of this for the sole purpose of convincing you. I am not looking for validation and to have my identity accepted by the world. I know who I am. I have been fine without the world knowing. Over the last few years there has been something growing inside of me, and now is the time for it to come out. Much the same way that I can't keep quiet when there is a song inside me that needs to come out. I ignored it for a while, and all it did was continue to grow. I can't keep this to myself anymore. It is my time, and I will not walk away from this anymore. I don't know what the master plan is, but I do know that I have to do this. I feel it in my soul.

I am an entertainer, so I obviously do hope that you enjoy it. I do hope that you believe me, but that is out of my control. You have read this far, so something has piqued your interest. During this process, I have found what I am looking for, and I hope that you do the same.

Now here is what I do have. I have three birth certificates, two from Texas and one from Louisiana. People went to a lot of effort to cover up where I came from. I have a birth certificate that shows that I was born to my adopted parents in Louisiana. I have a birth certificate from Texas that shows that I was born in Texas to my adopted parents. The funny thing is that my adopted parents were born and lived and always lived in Louisiana. Why go to Texas to give birth to me? I have a certificate of vital record from Texas that indicates my birth and that I have two older sisters, also born to my adopted parents. These are Emma and Becky, my maternal sisters. The Texas birth certificate is to cover over the restricted closed file that has my first birth certificate. This is the birth certificate that my birth mom traveled to Texas to retrieve in 2004. My birth mom and my father are the only two people that can access this file. In this file is the only accurate birth certificate. This birth certificate shows my mother as Zona Marie and my father as Elvis Aaron Presley. And people wonder why it took me so long to figure out who I am. How many birth certificates do you have? And I bet at times even you wondered if you were adopted into the family of circus freaks that you were growing up with.

I have a letter from a retired judge named Fred Sexton. Fred was just starting out his distinguished career in 1962. At the time, Fred was the clerk for Tom Staggs. Fred was the clerk that handled the private adoption of me and my sisters. He still remembers it to this day, as this letter will show.

JOHN DENNIS SMITH

May 13, 2011

Dear John Dennis,

Thank you for contacting me in this matter. I will do my best to recall after all these years. I do, however, remember the transaction of your adoption in our office many years ago. To the best of my knowledge Tom Staggs was the acting judge at the time of your adoption to Ira Dee and Etta Smith, your great aunt and uncle, on E.P.'s side of the family.

At the time of your adoption I was new in law and an assistant to Tom and aided in some of the paperwork. The adoption of you and your sisters was done in Tom's "Private Chambers" and is still today a much a golden memory in my mind and heart knowing that someone cared so much to take on not one, but three children. It was a high point of my start in law. I hope that I can assist you in looking for all of the truths you are searching for.

So the answer to the million dollar question after all these years is that, yes, I believe by the information I was handed then, the memories and number of tearing conversations with your birth mother as she was then, and still is, a close friend, that you are the son of E.P. without any doubt in my mind or heart..

I hope this will be of help to you in your endeavor and if you need me please do not hesitate to call me. I am, and will always be, here for you in any way I can be of help. I am glad you are taking the steps to show us all what has been in waiting for too long.

God Bless You
Your Friend,

Fred C. Sexton, Jr., Esquire

I have a letter from Ed Haun, a gentleman that was on the periphery of my life and has been in the background, observing what was transpiring in my life. It reads like this:

January 26, 2009

Ed Haun

Dear John D,

I thank you for your call as well has your mother's. I will be talking to you very soon. I hope that in your endeavor in this life task will be successful and that you will stand strong in your decision.

Let me take this opportunity to let you know I am happy that you have decided to move forward in your life long dream and know that myself and others around me will do all we can to help you in any way you may see fit. It has been our thoughts for a number of years that you go after your dream as it was, and would have been, your father's dream for you to succeed.

If you find you need me or anything else to help in this matter please don't hesitate to call me anytime at my direct number and I would hope you will use it any time you feel necessary.

With love and our Watchful eye,

Edward Haun

I have pictures and accounts of my life and of my mother's life from people that are close to both of us and were also close to Elvis. I have an e-mail conversation with HT at the passing of Sherrill Nielsen.

From:
To:
Date: Fri, December 10, 2010 2:44:25 PM
Cc:
Subject: Re: Sherrill Nielsen

Thanks John,

Now you are going to have to "step up" and take the lead ... you were there from the beginning ... now you have to take the lead ... get it going and let's do as much work as possible with you singing ... get it done ... all it takes is a little $$ and who knows, it might be just around the next bend in the road ... :-)

All the best,
HT

----- Original Message -----
From: John Smith
To: MusicCity
Sent: Friday, December 10, 2010 3:35 PM
Subject: Re: Sherrill Nielsen

Dear HT,
   I am with tears in my eyes and a void in my heart thinking of the many memories that we never think of until we have someone close pass away.
   I know right now you are feeling the loss, more so, than me as your friend of so many years has left us here.
   Know that after his strong and fearless battle with this life he is now in a better place. We can now look at the great songs, the great voice the great man. He will in all our lives stay as if he is here by being in our hearts. I remember one of the first times I meet Sherrill at Printers Alley and Profets Club. the times I spent learning from the 2 masters in my music and watching as you and he so strongly worked together and made what I know now was the best music I have and will ever hear. I have a egale neckless that Sherrill took off his neck and gave me just because I admired it. I will cherish. I remember the bed spread he gave me when he found out at my apartment that I didnt have one it was so thick and sheep skin i think..
   I remember putting on that big fur coat Elvis gave him he laughed as it was so big but I could and now even feel the warmth of it as I am telling you about it. I remember watching as back then me this boy, who with such honor I was a part of just seeing him sing. These and more I will always keep close and feel how lucky to know the singer, the voice but mostly the "Man" .   I will always know in my heart I sing today as I do because of you and because of Sherrill. You both have allowed me the "honor" of your teaching and guidence and I will be forever greatful.   I say all of that to simply say to you and to Sherrill even now " Thank you for all you are and have been in my life, yesterday, today and tomorrow. forever.

                    We will all miss him and truly we feel the loss, but know He is forever in our hearts and as you know, He's watching us still,   "as we LIVE and LET LIVE".
   I love you man my heart is with you and will always be ....

From: MusicCity
To: John Dennis Smith
Sent: Fri, December 10, 2010 1:14:53 PM

This is all part of my heritage. I am proud of who I am and of where I come from and of who my friends are. Please know this. I am not doing this to convince anyone of anything. I am telling the story of my life. If you find interest in it and believe it, that's great. If you think that I am trying to make a name for myself and take advantage, go ahead. I will tell you this. If my goal was just to make money off this, I would have done it a long, long time ago with a lot more sequins on my jumpsuits.

Living as John Smith

After hearing about parts of some of my life, people shake their heads and ask me what is left to do. I have lived so much life in the last fifty-one years that if everything were to end today, I would die a happy man. I have lived my life with few regrets. It has been an amazing adventure. If I had only experienced a portion of what has happened in my life, it would be more than most other people live in two lifetimes. I have lived every moment of it, and it is a good life.

Now don't get the idea that I am winding down. I only know one way to live. To keep looking forward to what is coming. Some people live their lives in reverse, looking back in regret over all of the things that they wished that they had done or keep trying to still live on the glories of yesterday. There aren't many chances that I did not take. I have always looked forward to the coming days because I firmly believe that my best days are still coming. They are on the way, and I am prepared to greet them with a smile, whistling all the while. Hey, that rhymes. Maybe I should write a song.

Here are just some of my stories. Some of my stories happened under the watchful eye of those around me in keeping the promise they made to my dad. A great many of these happened on my own. My friends joke that they can't take me anywhere, that I don't know someone, or that I at least have a friend in common with.

I have had so many experiences in my life that are beyond the norm. For me, it is just another day in the life. Telling about the many events in my life is often met with incredulity and sometimes more than a little skepticism. I had told a buddy of mine about my first show with Lawrence Welk. It was the Elks Convention at the San Diego Convention Center. I was onstage, just me and a guitar. I was late. Not because of me. I was there, and ready to go. Standing behind the curtain. Nobody could open the curtain, because they had forgotten to arrange for an employee of the union of curtain pullers to be present. It took forty-five minutes to get someone there who was qualified to flip the switch that would open the curtain. Finally at long last, the curtain opened, and thousands of people were expecting me to burst into song. I froze. This was not the Louisiana Hayride back home or any of the other stages that I was used to. Thousands of eyes were looking at me that I had never seen before. I froze. I am standing in the loneliest spot in the world. In the middle of the stage frozen, with the spotlight on me. This is the first time in my life that I have ever had stage fright, and I had waited for my biggest audience ever for it to happen. I stood there like a rock until a man walked over to me from offstage, tapped me on the shoulder, and said, "It's okay, son. You can go ahead and sing for these nice people." The place erupted in laughter. They thought it was part of the show, and suddenly I was fine. I am now where I belong: onstage with a microphone and a crowd before me. I was no longer scared. I was home. I sang my heart out and loved every minute of it. I had told Rich this story. He has heard most of my stories during the life of our friendship. Rich relayed this story to his cousin. His cousin lived across the street from Ken Delo, who was a prominent member of the Lawrence Welk Show. After telling Ken about me and my time on the show, Ken responded by saying he had no memory of me ever being around or even on the show. The skepticism sets in. The cousin told Rich to be careful, I may be pulling his leg. Rich replied to his cousin, "Don't doubt Johnny. He has been right too many times."

There were two things that they did not know. As is the custom in the South, many times a young man goes by his middle name growing up. I don't know why, it just happens. For most of my growing-up years, people knew me as Dennis. The second is that there was a Lawrence Welk TV show and a traveling live show that was used to entertain audiences and groom performers for the television show. I was on the live show. It also kept live performances from interfering with the taping of the TV show. About a year after this exchange between my friend and his cousin, I was staying with Rich, and I was at his cousin's for a block party barbeque. Sure enough, Ken Delo was there too. It is now time for Johnny to have a little fun. I start talking to Ken about the show and his time spent there. As the conversation progresses, I start to mention things about the show and the people there, that only someone that was also there would know about. "Remember the old airplane we used to fly on? The one that was so loud that if you didn't get there early, you had to sit over the wing, and you couldn't talk to anyone? Remember the time we landed at Burbank, and we landed so hard that one of the windows popped out into one of the ladies' laps? Remember one of the places that we stayed where the TV came sliding up out of the cabinet that it was in? Remember how Lawrence never paid for anything?"

He keeps asking how I know. I keep asking him if he remembers certain events. He is getting more and more curious and dumbfounded, and I keep on going. I finally ask him if he remembers that time at the convention center in San Diego for the Elk's Club, when he walked onstage and tapped that boy on the shoulder that had stage fright and told him it was okay to go ahead and sing. He said, "You mean little Dennis? How do you know about little Dennis?"

I spread my arms out and grinned, "I am little Dennis."

The collective jaws dropped, and Ken wrapped me up in his arms with tears in his eyes. I love this stuff. This is what my life is like. It happens over and over again. You may want to think twice and maybe, just maybe, reserve judgment in case parts of my story seem too strange to be true. I have more "little Dennis" moments than most people have memorable moments.

I imagine that people are interested in my life mainly because of my Elvis connection. This is understandable. I am still intrigued by him and all that he accomplished. I would love to sit down with him and find out what he was thinking. I would love to know the whys of what he did and how he lived. Not the stories about him, but what he was thinking. What did he think about me? Why he took care of me and my mom? How he kept an eye on me? If he ever heard me sing? These are questions that may never be answered. I have my own ideas in my heart about the man, and I have the stories from his friends and, most of all, stories from my mom. I also have more unseen, unreleased, and unknown items from the life of Elvis than most people can imagine. Each one comes with its own story attached to it. Here are just a few of them:

- The trust fund that Elvis had a hand in setting up for me.
- Baby pictures with Elvis holding me.
- Family photos of Elvis when he was a child.
- Pictures of me onstage with Elvis when I was a child.
- Song lyrics handwritten by Elvis.
- Test pressings of Elvis records, some where Elvis handwrote a message on the jacket.
- Notes and e-mails from those close to Elvis making reference to the connection between Elvis and myself.
- Crystal goblets from the Graceland collection.
- Childhood pictures of Elvis.
- The flag that was mailed to me that was supposed to be on the casket of Elvis.
- Elvis recording a song about my mom.
- Vernon Presley's pocketknife.
- Gladys Presley's change purse.
- The maid that took care of Elvis also took care of me.
- Gladys Presley's family Bible.
- A lifetime of comparisons to Elvis when I sing.

All of this is only a portion of what I have in my possession or have access to from the people that love both Elvis and me.

I enjoy having these items and more around me. They tell me where I came from. They are part of my history. I appreciate the sentimental meanings of these items. The value to me is only sentimental. They are not practical. I guess I could sell them, but then I would spend the money, and I would be left with no money and no heirlooms. No, I will keep them for what they mean to me. They are part of my family history. I like knowing that no one else has what I have. It reminds me that I am special to my family, even if it was not publicly acknowledged. I belong to a family. That in itself is a good feeling. Instead of using my family treasures to build a shrine to what is past, I have chosen a different route with my life. I take the security of knowing that I have a family that I belong to, and I use the strength I gain from that to go and explore my own path.

You will not believe all the stories that I can tell. Again, I enjoy it, and I fully expect these crazy things to happen. I am just being me, and it happens over and over and over again. Many of my friends used to not be able to believe it. After I keep being proved right, time after time, they just shrug their shoulders, laugh, and say, "Of course it happened."

Here is one of my stories that covers five states. One day in Dallas, a friend of mine asked me to come along with him to the home of Phil Mims. Phil was very successful in a multilevel marketing business called Excel. My friend Randy was going to check it out and see if it was something that he wanted to pursue. I came along so I could advise Randy on what I thought of the whole deal. Here is the first coincidence. I had just started a Christian music group, and I named it His Dominion.

Phil Mims lived on Dominion Street in the Dallas area. It is a small thing, I know. In my life, I never know when the small things are going to turn into big things. We go in and meet Phil. By the way, after this adventure and a few others, Phil ends up being a mentor to me and also serves on an advisory board for me. On this day, we meet Phil. We sit down and talk business and life for a couple of hours. I am enjoying myself. I always like meeting new people. And Phil has some good stories of his own to tell. We have been there for a while, and Phil says that he is hungry, so it is time to eat. He pulls out some hot dogs and makes lunch.

As we are eating, Phil makes a comment about going to Colorado as he talks around the bite of hot dog in his mouth. I don't catch all of what he says, but I hear Colorado. This is another thing about me that leads to some of my misadventures. I don't always hear what I think I hear when I say yes to something. I perk up. I love Colorado. I ask him when he is going and why. He tells us that he is going the next day. His friend Old Charlie is not feeling well. Old Charlie has a ranch, and he can't get up and around right then. He needs to have his hay baled and brought into the barn, and he needs to bring the cattle in before winter. Then he asks around another bite if we want to come. Right here is one of the reasons I have these experiences. I say yes. You can't go if you don't say yes. I don't have anything going at the moment, so I say yes. I am open to the possibilities. I have many things that do not work out and leave me wondering why I fall for the same things over and over again. This does not keep me from trying. When it works out, it is a lot of fun. This is why I keep doing these crazy things.

The next day we leave for Colorado, riding along with Phil. The trip was uneventful; most of the time was spent getting to know each other and talking about Phil's business. As we approach Ridgway, Colorado, where Phil also has a home, I have heard all there is to hear about Excel. I tell him that I like his phone business idea. I don't want to sign up or anything, but I will sell it for him. In fact, I will show him what I can do, and I will sell it to someone at the first place we stop. Phil gives me an understanding smile and tells me that he doesn't mean to brag, but he knows the people here, and he has this town pretty well sewn up. I tell him not to worry and just see what John can do.

Our first stop was for gas. While Phil was getting gas, I walked inside and saw that the lady behind the counter was crying as she was hanging up the phone. I am curious by nature and do not like to see people sad, so I ask her what is wrong. I don't mean to pry, but I noticed that she was crying. She tells me through her tears and sniffles that she was talking to her mom. She misses her mom and grandmother very much, but she can't afford to call them from home because she can't afford a long-distance plan. She has to wait until she comes to work to use the phone there to call her mom. I ask her that if I had a way that she could talk to them, would she be interested. I explained to her how Excel worked. I thought she was going to hug me. I step to the door and holler out to Phil. "Hey, come in here and bring one of those application packets with you!" I stand there grinning like I just won first prize while Phil walks her through the application. I love this. I get to prove me right and help someone in need at the same time. I also get to see the look of disbelief on Phil's face.

After having to answer a ton of questions about how did I do what I just did, we finally arrive at Old Charlie's ranch. As we are getting settled in, we meet Greg Beck. Greg is Phil's friend from California. Greg is wearing a polo shirt and loafers. I am thinking, *Great, we have one cowboy. That's me. Two guys that think they are cowboys, and one guy dressed for golf. This should be fun.* We all load up and get started. Before we start on the hay, we have to bring the cattle in. We stop to get some equipment out in a field. While we are loading up, suddenly we hear a loud roar. We all freeze and then look up. It's a bear coming right for us. I did not just ride sixteen hours to get eaten by a bear. I look around for the gun. Luckily, Randy was right by the truck where the gun was. He grabbed the gun and shot the bear.

We could go home right now and have a great story to tell. And my knees were wanting to take me home. We were all still shaking at our close call. We haven't even started work yet. What is the rest of this adventure going to bring? We proceed to bring in the cows and then spend the next three days baling and hauling hay. There were no further incidents, only acres and acres of hay that seemed to go on forever. By the third day, I was almost wishing for another bear so there would have been something to break up the day and to take my mind off how tired my arms, back, legs, and shoulders were. We were beat tired, but we got it done and saved Old Charlie's place for the winter. When you work beside someone for a time, you learn about their character. I learned that Phil is a good-hearted, hardworking man of his word. He went to great lengths to help his neighbor. It is always good to make a new friend with his qualities.

It was now the end of the week, and Sunday was coming. Phil told us that we would all be going to church with him and Old Charlie. At church the next morning, Phil told Pastor Joe that I was a singer and had my own group. I am noticing that every person that I meet in this town seems to have a prequel to their name. Old Charlie, Uncle Bob, Pastor Joe. And on it goes. Pastor Joe said that if Phil thought that I was something special, then maybe I would sing a song for them that morning. Almost every time I am asked to sing a song, it is never just one song. It almost always turns into two or three songs, and then a lot of handshaking, backslapping, and then, "You know, I have a cousin/sister/uncle/nephew that is a good singer. Maybe you have heard of him/her/them."

Pastor Joe introduces me during the service, and I proceed to sing a song. Then I sing another song. Then before I am allowed to sit back down, I sing another song. Finally, I am done. I enjoy this. It is part of what I do. After the service is over, there is a lot of handshaking and backslapping, and then I meet Uncle Bob, who has experience in the music business. Of course he does, it happens all the time. I meet Uncle Bob, and he does have some experience in music. Uncle Bob has a benefit program that he does that involves music. He records children when they sing in church or his own grandkids when they sing. He takes these recordings into the studio and cleans them up and makes copies of them on cassette tapes. Uncle Bob then takes the tapes and distributes them to shut-ins and old folks' homes. He says that it brightens the days of older people to hear children singing.

That is a great idea. I ask him how he funds this endeavor and how he makes it work. Uncle Bob tells me that he does it. He takes care of it and does it because he wants to and it helps people. We talk about it some more until Uncle Bob invites us over for lunch. Now I have just met Uncle Bob at a small-town church. He seems like an ordinary nice man with a big heart. When I see his house, I think that he is a nice man with a big heart and a whole lot of money. I start asking questions, and this is how I learn the story of Uncle Bob.

Uncle Bob Hunter was the owner of Hunter Tools, along with his brother. After years of making tools for mechanics, Uncle Bob's brother wanted out of the business. Uncle Bob bought out his brother for about ten thousand dollars. After this, Bob was trying to think of ways to expand his business. He wondered if there was a way to sell his tools directly to people at home and not just to mechanics. A friend of Bob's owned a successful catalog store. This is how we used to order things to get shipped to our homes before there was online shopping. It was done over a telephone line, and we used a catalog instead of a website. Bob went to his friend and told him about the idea. His friend who owned a Sears store told him that this was a crafty idea and did not see any reason why his high-quality tools would not sell. And this is how Uncle Bob Hunter changed the name of Hunter tools to Craftsman Tools. And the rest is history. I guess Uncle Bob did not need anyone's help to go make cassette tapes to share with others.

The afternoon is wearing on as we continue to talk about life and businesses. At some point, the conversation turns to recycling and reusing the resources that we have. Uncle Bob turns to me and says that I need to meet his neighbor. Okay, who's next? I have already encountered more than I expected. I thought I was coming to Colorado to play cowboy for three days. Uncle Bob's neighbor is teaching something called ecolonomics, which is the economics of ecology. He was going green before there was a green to go to. Uncle Bob gets up and says, "Let me call him."

He comes back a minute later and tells us to get up and grab our stuff. "We are going next door to meet Chester. You know, Chester from *Gunsmoke*." I am not puzzled very often, but right now I am. We drive next door. In this part of the world, next door can be several miles. We get to the door, and Uncle Bob hollers out to the resident to hurry up and let us in.

"Hold your horses! Hold your horses. I'm coming," we hear back in a familiar voice. The door opens, and I am staring at Dennis Weaver. You know, Chester on the TV show *Gunsmoke*. What in the world am I doing standing on the front porch of the famous actor Dennis Weaver? This is turning into quite a day. Wait, it gets better.

Dennis invites us in, and we spend the next few minutes asking the usual questions about his acting and looking at memorabilia from his career. We then sit down in his living room. While I am still taking all of my surroundings in, Uncle Bob launches into ecolonomics. Dennis Weaver joins in tells me all about the details of ecolonomics. He then proudly tells me that you can now get degrees in this area at five different colleges. I have never heard of this, so I ask Dennis, "How would I know?"

He looks puzzled and wants to know how I would know what.

"How would I know that I can get a degree in this field?"

He and Uncle Bob exchanged looks. They had never heard this question before. "You just go to the school, and you find out about it," was the uncertain reply.

I proceed to tell them that I do not think that this is a good marketing model. "You want to attract people before they get to college. Once they get to college, you have to talk them out of their planned major and get them to switch to yours. Why don't you reach them before they get to college? That makes more sense to me."

It is obvious that Dennis has not thought of this approach. He wants to know how do they do that. It seems so obvious to me. You teach it to them in middle school and high school. Maybe even elementary school. Dennis wants to know how we do that. I notice that now he is using the word *we*.

I tell him, "*We* do this by developing teacher units and getting it into school curriculum."

"How do we do that?"

"We do that by writing and publishing a curriculum and then getting it into the schools."

Uncle Bob and Dennis look at each other and discuss how they do not know how to do that. They then turn to me, and they both ask if I can do that.

"Yes, I can. I have a friend that writes curriculum for the Dallas-area schools. I can do that with her. Her name is Kathy McMillan." I tell them that I can do it, but I will need to have Dennis available for speaking engagements and that we also need to make a video about the project for times that Dennis is not available.

They want to know when I can start and what I need.

This is my life. I leave Texas to go and bale some hay. I come back with Dennis Weaver and the owner of Craftsman Tools as my new friends. And not just friends.

We are now business partners. I also have a new high-profile project to work on.

When I get back to Texas, I get together with Kathy. We form Smith-McMillan Publishing and create the curriculum. It goes into schools, and Dennis begins to promote it. I had no idea that this kind of project was waiting for me. I had never dreamed of writing school curriculum. I didn't even like school when I was there. This all happened because when Old Charlie needed help, I said yes.

I once heard a story about a man that went up to heaven. God was showing him around heaven, and they saw a huge storehouse. God told him that this storehouse was filled with opportunities and blessings that people never asked for while they were on earth. Most people live life on the cautious side, and I can understand why. I look at life differently. I would rather fall flat on my face than miss out on the blessings that God has planned for me. I saw an advertisement on a bus stop one day as I was driving by. It said that if you never use your backup plan, you have lived life to safe.

This is my life. Elvis enters my life on a continual basis as well. As I have stated before, I do not go looking for it. It comes to me in various forms. I was singing at a reception for a lady. It was not a formal thing. There was a piano player there. He and I began to talk. He handed me a microphone and asked me to sing something. I did, and then another and another. A friend of mine was talking to the lady that was hosting the reception when her nephew came up to her. "This is a great reception, auntie. The food is great, this place is beautiful, and look, you have Elvis up there singing." For the record, I was singing Sinatra at the time.

I have often had people tell me as I have been singing that with my voice, I would sound great singing Elvis songs. Would I please do some of his songs?

Where I live, there is a local watering hole that the locals meet at every afternoon. As we were wrapping up the book recently, I was down there enjoying my usual afternoon ice tea and two-dollar chicken wings. I was talking to my friend TC. TC is quite a character. He trains and rides buffalo. I can't even begin to imagine what it is like to do trick riding bareback on a thousand-pound beast, but he does. He does it well too. The fact that he is still alive, with all of his body parts intact, is proof of how good he is. Rich and I had just found out when the book would be going into production, and I was very excited about it. I was telling TC about it, and I mentioned the date. A gentleman that I had never seen before was sitting next to me at the bar. He nudged me and told me that he heard me mention that date, and that's his anniversary. What is happening then? I am downplaying it because I have no idea who this guy is. I tell him that I have a book coming out. He says that he wants a copy. "You don't even know what it's about. How do you know you want one?"

"I just want one. What is it about?" is his reply.

I tell him that I am a musician, and the book is about my life. "I have had some interesting experiences in my life."

"Well then, I want one. I am a musician by hobby, and I worked for Capitol Records for years in Chicago."

"Really? I was on Capitol Records for a time in Nashville." Another connection to a stranger that I have never seen before. We trade a few names to see if we are both for real. We end up realizing that we know some of the same people in the business. This new friend pauses for a moment as he sizes me up. Then he says, "I guess next you're going to tell me that you know some of the Elvis people."

TC leans around me and tells him, "Oh, you have done it now!"

I have barely scratched the surface of stories that I have.

There is still the night I sang for Mary Bonham, the lady that owned JB Weld. She gave me ten thousand dollars and told me to go get my music out. When I expressed concern about the size of the check, she told me not to worry about it. She spends more than that on horse feed every month.

I haven't told you about meeting John Denver in a recording studio. About growing a friendship with him and playing with him onstage and helping to engineer a record for him. Years later playing some of his music and having his father-in-law come up to me and introduce himself. He then tells me that I sing John Denver songs like I had known John.

The weekend that I was sailing my boat around the Bahamas and had some friends with me. Lita Ford the rock star wouldn't use the bathroom in the v-berth up front in the sailboat, so I had to run my new boat aground so that she could go to the bathroom on dry land.

The time I spent singing for the Mandrell Sisters band.

The time that I was the only white guy in the Victory Chapel singing for and with the bishop TD Jakes.

The months that I spent in Bandera, Texas, the cowboy capital of the world.

How I went to Bandera to try and escape the greatest tragedy in my life.

How I got a John Smith Day in Bandera.

About how I rode a horse into a bar. (Yes, I have pictures.)

About riding on the cattle drive from Bandera to Calgary and arriving there for the Calgary Stampede, which takes place every year.

Spending three years on the rodeo circuit and winning roping championships.

My first and last times riding bulls. I don't remember the last time. I do remember the helicopter ride and the stitches in my face from it.

Going to India on a mission trip and being the only man to be allowed to sing inside an Indian prison to the inmates. Coming back from the trip and being interviewed by the FBI about what was really going on during that trip. On a mission trip to Bulgaria, having our musical equipment stolen. One year later receiving a phone call from the thief, asking for forgiveness. I received this call right before I was to go onstage at a church. I was with the same pastor that I took the trip to Bulgaria with. He was with me when the equipment was stolen.

The day that I heard the story of a young crippled girl at a hospital and wrote the song "Please Let Me Love You."

Having the amazing opportunity to play with the Christian recording artist Rich Mullins shortly before he died in a tragic accident.

There are these stories and much, much more. But it is late. I am tired, and I am going to bed.

Why Now?

Why now and what now? The first is the question I am often asked. The second is the question that I most often ask myself.

Why now? Why did I wait all these years to make all of this public? There are many reasons. This book has been a long time coming for many reasons. It has not been an easy story to tell. Not for the obvious reasons, but for a deeply personal reason. In the telling of my story, I have to open up about myself. I have learned to keep my guard up to protect myself. Not many people get to see the me who is not the performer. I am naturally shy about myself. I enjoy what others have to say about me, but I am reluctant to talk about my own talent. The talent that I have received is a gift. I did not work to develop my vocal cords. They were given to me. I have worked to improve myself as a songwriter; however, I can't control the ideas and pictures that come into my head and come out as lyrics and melodies that touch people's hearts. It is hard to describe the process. It is like me trying to describe how I breathe. It just happens as a natural part of everyday nature. In my world, singing and writing are as natural and as commonplace as walking and breathing. One of the things that Rich does, is build guitars. He and I have had many discussions about this. He is the same way with woodworking as I am with writing a song. When he holds a piece of raw wood in his hands, he knows what it is going to be and how it will look when it is finished. He says that the wood tells him what to do. And then each new guitar sparks more ideas for more guitars. I am the same way with a song. Sometimes I labor for days, and sometimes I can't keep it inside of me. The words and melody will come out of me in a rush. On those days, I can't write fast enough to keep up with what is in my head. One day, my band and I were in a studio in Dallas recording some new material. We had finished all that we hoped to accomplish that day when the recording engineer told us that we had some more time. Was there anything else that we wanted to do? I love being in the studio. It is one of the most creative places to be. If you ask me if I want to keep going, my answer is yes. You never know what will come out of it. You never know when that magical moment will happen when you capture something that lasts for years. I said yes, but I needed to use the restroom first. I went to the restroom and wrote "Raining on My Heart" in ten minutes. An hour later, it had been recorded. One of the moments that just clicked. Here is what I wrote:

One more line, and I could write
The story of the way I feel
The day we met and fell in love
I guess it's over now I see

And even though the skies in Texas
They stay blue most of the time
If you leave me, clouds will gather

And it starts raining on my heart

I watched you go as you drive away
Still I tried to hold on
To what we had
Honey, you and I
Those memories of yesterday

And even though the skies in Texas
They stay blue most of the time
If you leave me, clouds will gather
And it starts raining on my heart

Storm clouds rolling in
With the Texas night
Those teardrops turn to rain
And they keep falling from my eyes

And even though the skies in Texas
They stay blue most of the time
If you leave me, clouds will gather
And it starts raining on my heart
It starts raining on my heart.

Why haven't I gone public before now? There are several reasons. These reasons are all personally motivated. I have a good life. I live an intentionally simple life. In the course of my life, I have had it all. I have had excess and great success. I have had nothing and no place to lay my head. I have been married. I have been single. I have no complaints about my life. It has for the most part been my life. The life that I have chosen to have. How many people can say that? I have made great friends. I have lived many amazing experiences. I have tasted fame and have seen the price that it demands when you are not prepared for it. I have not had to live my life under the microscope like my father did. I am free to enjoy my life and choose what I want to do and where I want to go and who to spend time with. These are all things that my father lost in the course of his success.

Elvis made the comment that he would have to die to get any kind of freedom back. He was part of a huge machine that was feeding him and feeding off him. Fame is a double-edged sword filled with givers and takers, and the takers are hungry and demanding. They are eager to wring every last drop out of you until you can't go on. Then they cast you aside and turn to the next big thing. I have experienced enough of this on the smaller scale to recognize that I don't want to play this game anymore.

John Denver, Dennis Weaver, and I had many private conversations about this topic. In a way, I am grateful to Elvis for protecting me from what was ultimately his downfall. The people close to him saw it and took steps to protect me from the same fate that was waiting for Elvis.

Because of what Elvis did for me, either on purpose or inadvertently, I got to have a life. The kind of life I chose to have. It was not always easy; however, the choices were mine. I am old enough now to know what I want and what I don't want in my life. Revealing my story is not going to thrust me into the spotlight like the wide-eyed child I used to be. I am fifty-one years old. It is a lot of miles and a lot of years since my first night onstage at the Lawrence Welk Show in Shreveport, Louisiana. My demographics have changed. They are not the same as Justin Bieber. It is more likely the parents and, even though it pricks the pride of my own vanity to admit it, the grandparents too.

When I was starting out, I never would have imagined that my target audience would be the same age group that Lawrence Welk was targeting. Tell me that God does not have a sense of humor. As comedian Bill Cosby used to say, God has eternity. He can wait thirty years for the punch line. That is where I find myself now. I laugh at myself, and even though I make fun of it, I am glad for the generation that will be interested in my story. I will probably not be mobbed in public by teenage girls like my father was. I actually get to be in public. I am glad that I have had the good fortune to have people around me protecting me from having too much too soon. The success rate of child stars is not a good one. I'm not talking about financial success. I'm talking about quality of life. Many child stars have everything and end up with nothing, financially and socially. In many cases, this was because they were unprepared to handle it or they listened to the takers. I never wanted to have it all. A close friend of mine told me that the happiest that he has ever seen me is in a picture where I am elbow-deep in cleaning fish on a river in Louisiana. We were talking one day about growing up in the spotlight and why do so many young people go sideways and mess up their lives. I feel that sometimes people act out because they are trying to find the true person inside of them. The only person that they know is the person that they show to the world, and it is not who they are in their soul. They are trying to find what they keep missing.

I enjoy the simple life. I always have. If money was going to change that in me, it already would have. I don't have the burden of trying to find out who I am while the world watches my every move. I know who I am. I have had the time I need to explore who I am and what I want from life. Part of my answer to why now is that I have been given much in my life, and I am at the place where I am ready to give back to life out of what I have been blessed with. It is said that life isn't truly lived until it is given away. Many people in the public eye have their lives taken from them by others. It is a completely different perspective when you get to decide how much of yourself to give away. Winston Churchill said, "You make a living by what you make. You make a life by what you give away." This is where I now find myself. I don't need anything, but I do realize that I have something to offer.

Another part of why I have waited for this time is that for many years, there was a strong culture around Elvis. The message of this culture is that "nobody messes with the King." This message was the mantra that those in the circle of Elvis lived by every day. Elvis was such a powerful figure and had a strong personality that drew the loyalty of those that surrounded him. This was a time when a man's word was his bond, and those close to Elvis might have just as well sworn a blood oath to keep his and my secrets. This culture of secrecy was at a time when celebrities were revered and built up by the media that covered them. There were very few expose pieces going around. This secrecy protected me and held me back at the same time. I was never directly forbidden from pursuing avenues in my career, but I was guided and directed away from some areas that I wanted to pursue to expand my career and exposure. I don't blame anyone around me for this. With time comes perspective. I now look back on the actions of those that were around me from the position of a parent that is trying to protect a child from possible harm. They were more interested in protecting me from the pitfalls instead of daring me to dream and reach the heights that were waiting to be found. If I had achieved greater success as a young man, it could have very well led to unwanted questions about where I came from and the crowd of Elvis people that were surrounding me and my life.

Protecting the King kept me and others quiet for decades. I believe that enough time has gone by and that the world is ready to hear and hopefully would enjoy my perspective of life from my side of the Elvis phenomenon. I have a letter from HT that I have kept for years. Back in 1998, I floated the idea of telling the world who I was, and I received a handwritten note back from him telling me all I needed to know. I find it ironic that I keep receiving Dear John letters. This one said the following:

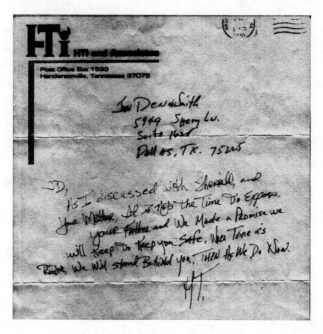

That was then and this is now. And this is the time.

I believe in my heart that we are created for certain moments in our lives that will define us, and we have the opportunity to define ourselves. This is one of these times in my life, as I will explain later in this chapter.

What I want to achieve is just as important as what I hope to avoid. What I don't want to do is to exploit the fame of Elvis, as so many others have, in books and in costume. I am not an Elvis impersonator. Don't get me wrong, I love the many Elvis impersonators that I have met. They are a lot of fun and are in the business of honoring and remembering my dad. Every time that I or one of my close friends see an Elvis impersonator, we have to get a picture taken with them. I am gathering quite a catalog of father-and-son pictures. It is hilarious. It is all in good-natured fun. They are paying tribute to my dad after all of these years. I think it is great.

One day it looked like we were on the verge of a breakthrough with taking my story public, and a man involved in the process wanted to meet me at the local cowboy watering hole. He told me that this was a big deal and for me to keep everything quiet. This was not the time to draw attention to myself. I was waiting for him when he arrived, sitting on a bench at a table, right next to an Elvis impersonator in full costume, who just happened to be there. I caught his eye and saw the look of shock on his face. I yelled out across the room. "Hey! Do you want to meet my dad?" It was too perfect. I could not resist.

I am not an Elvis impersonator. I am John Smith, and like my father, I love to sing. Art is its own reward. I have sat back and watched over the years as people have come forward and made their claims to be offspring of Elvis. This is their one and only claim to fame. I have watched in amazement at a world that is eager to grab on to anything that is Elvis and will temporarily gravitate toward things that are not real. They do make the news for a little while. I believe that the loyal fans of Elvis deserve more than these as a reward for the decades of faithfulness. The timing is right. Lisa Marie has recently revealed that she is ready to stop running from her heritage as the child of Elvis and embrace what that heritage means. Elvis has been gone for thirty-five years and is still in everyday conversation. He is still incredibly popular and is generating tens of millions of dollars every year. I have already received the gift of life from a good man. I desire nothing more from him or his estate. I have never asked for anything and never will. I want what I have always wanted: to let the world hear that this boy can sing.

Being an actual child of Elvis gives me my genetic makeup, and that is a gift that is meant to be shared. I would be foolish and a liar if I were to say that the popularity of Elvis did not play a part in my decision. It is obvious that the world still wants Elvis, and I look forward to the opportunity to meet fans and to share my story with them. I have said before that my interest is not to trade on the name of Elvis, but to add to what he started. As a parent, I also know that the dream of a parent is to see their children be better at life and to surpass them in success. I will never achieve what my father did. I will never change the world as he has. I can do the best I can with the talent I have. I want to honor him by achieving all that I can and see the continuation of his legacy. Most of all, I also want to honor the memory of the man that gave me life.

I also have my own legacy to leave behind. This became more real to me than ever in the summer of 2011. The story starts in April. Actually, the story starts in 1984 with the birth of my son Ross to me and my first wife. When Ross was four years old, I came home early one day and found out that who I thought was my best friend was really my wife's best friend. I walked in the door to find my new ex-best friend and my soon to be ex-wife in a compromising position. He was sitting in my recliner in his underwear. I mean, come on, not my recliner! She was coming out of the bedroom wearing lingerie. My son was playing on the floor. They were caught speechless, and my new ex–best friend was finding it even harder to speak with the barrel of my pistol in his mouth. Larry the Cable Guy says that "guns don't kill people, husbands that come home early kill people." I have no desire to inflict harm on anyone, but being crushed by the unimaginable scene I just walked into, I had to get out of there before I did something in the heat of passion that I would regret. I walked out, never to come back.

In retrospect, I wish I had thought more about what my leaving meant to my son. My adopted dad was good to me, but he had already raised his son from a previous marriage. I think that he felt his parenting days were done. He did not teach me about parenting while I was growing up. He was more about raising me to be a good person and to groom me for musical success. I did not know the pieces that I was missing by being adopted and not having my real dad there every day. I was also hurting so badly from this betrayal. I had given this man a job and welcomed him into my home. This was my repayment? I was angry with my wife as well, but he and I were like brothers. There are lines you just don't cross. I couldn't even imagine how many times he had looked me in the eye and known what he was doing, or planning on doing, to betray me. I left and couldn't go back. What ensued was one of the fastest breakups ever. I couldn't process the divorce papers fast enough, and they couldn't wait to get their marriage license as soon as our divorce was final.

After this I had little contact with my son. I tried for a while, but seeing them all together was too painful of a reminder to me. I do what I can to avoid uncomfortable and painful situations in my life. I wish that I had overcome this feeling in this situation for the sake of my son and for me. My ex-wife also kept persistently asking me to give up my parental rights so that the three of them and their new daughter could be a complete family. I felt completely discarded, like I didn't even exist anymore. Between all that and my life on the road, my contact with my son became a thing of the past. Any thoughts of reuniting with my son came to abrupt end when I got a call one fateful night. Ross would have been seventeen. It was my ex–mother-in-law telling me that Ross had been killed by a drunk driver in a traffic accident. She told me the town that it had happened in and the number of the police officer to call to get the details.

I was crushed. The weight of tragedy, loss, and regret was pressing down on me like nothing I had ever felt. Feeling numb and empty, I dialed the police office with shaking hands and heard the worst news of my life. A teenage boy had been killed in a collision with a drunk driver. The police officer could not release the names of those involved as he did not know who I was, and he needed to maintain privacy for the sake of the family. Once more I am on the outside looking in at my own son. My mother-in-law had told me that the service was taking place immediately, leaving me no time to make it back there. There was so much animosity between her and I that I didn't even think that I could face seeing her and the rest of them at this time. I turned away from them for the last time, now having nothing left to tie me to the hurtful reminder of my past. I disappeared into a bottle to try and forget and to not feel anything. Feelings and memories were my worst enemies at this time. I knew then and I know now that the bottle holds no answers for me. It was not the right thing to do or the right way to handle it. It is the way I chose, and I would have to deal with that later. For a brief time, it killed the memories. That was my only desire.

The thought never occurred to me that I was being lied to. I wish that it had. Trusting what people tell me has more than once cost me dearly. Even though I would classify my ex and her mom as close to the enemy category as one can get, I could not imagine that this story would be a fabrication. How could it be? Who would do such a thing? I cannot begin to tell you how much I regret not seeking further verification. The only thing I can say is that I was young and hurting so badly that I did not want to uncover any more pain.

Years later I found out the truth. Ross had been growing more and more upset about his homelife and his mom and had run away. His mom and grandmother were scared that he might run to me and wanted me as far away from the situation as possible. They had spent the last twelve years trying to make their own version of life and could not stand to see that come undone. They were scared of what would happen with Ross if some of their lies were uncovered, so they started another lie. They heard of a teenager being tragically killed in an accident and knew a police officer involved in the case. They told him of their plan to tell me that this had been my son and asked him to verify the facts of the accident, without releasing any names, when I called. He did, and I believed it. The officer did not lie to me. He just kept what he knew to himself. This was how I came to believe that I had lost my only son. This brings us to the spring of 2011.

In April of 2011, my attorney Jim Carroll and I decided to float the idea that there was a living, breathing son of Elvis. Jim has always told me that any kind of publicity is good. Let's see how the public reacts to it. He did go on to say that not all publicity is good publicity. There are reasonable limits, so we should try to demonstrate good judgment. We decided to start small, in the township of Egg Harbor, New Jersey, where Jim used to be the town solicitor. We met with the mayor, and he issued a proclamation, giving me my own day in Egg Harbor and naming it John Smith Presley day. I sang for a group of people, and there was a write-up in the local paper. It was the most talked about article in the town's history, with comments ranging from excitement to disinterest to skepticism. There was even a comment complaining that I was to blame for an unpaid bar tab in Kansas. This was pretty much what we expected. It didn't reach the state or national news, so we carried on with our lives and continued planning for the next step.

A couple of months later, I was with my friend Randy at a bar in Texas, getting ready to go onstage when my phone rings with an unfamiliar number. I know people all over the country that call me at strange times, so I answered it. It was a young lady calling. She asked me if I was the John Dennis Smith that used to live in Nashville and a few other places. I hesitantly answered yes. "What is this in regard to?"

She said that if I was this man that she was looking for, there was a young man wanting to get in touch with me. This young man thinks that he is my son. Would I be willing to speak with him?

I am freaked out and speechless and am about to walk onstage. I hand the phone to Randy and mumble for him to handle this. I know that it can't be true, and I have to regain my composure and go perform. I am thinking, *Great, I just went public with who my daddy is, and now people are going to start claiming to be my kid so they can get their fifteen minutes of fame.*

I am not sure I remember how, but I got through my set and got offstage. Randy gives me back my phone and tells me that this girl does not sound crazy. I call her back and find out that she is claiming to be the daughter of my ex and my ex–best friend. She claims that Ross is still alive and would like to find me. After my heart rate, my mind, and my sweat glands, all calm down, I tell her to go ahead and give this young man my number, and I will talk to him. I won't make any promises because my son has been dead for nine years, and I have not heard a thing from anyone during this time.

Now I am looking at my phone, wondering if this time it will bring a call that will change my life again, or will it just pull the scab off an old wound and reintroduce me to the old pain all over again. I don't know if it is worse to be waiting for it or to be surprised by the call. There it is! The phone is ringing! I take a couple of deep breaths and say, "Hello?" Now there is no going back.

"Is this John Smith?"

"Yes, it is. Is this Ross?"

A hesitant start to a reunion conversation, both of us hoping and wanting to know. Both of us having been hurt deeply by our past and not wanting to go back to those painful times. We both know what it is like to experience loss, and we don't want to leave ourselves open to feel that particular pain again. Once was too many. We are both holding back from revealing too much. Like poker players wondering what cards the other one is holding. I start by asking him a few questions about what he remembers. He answers mine and asks me his own questions. His responses and memories are close enough to be real. This is either an elaborate hoax or the real thing. I am cautious and skeptical. I now know how it feels to be on the other side of the question about who my daddy is. It is a bit unnerving. One more question pops into my mind as I have been trying to think of things that only my son as a young boy would know.

"Do you remember what I gave you on the day that turned into the last day that I ever saw you?" I waited without breathing for his answer.

After a short pause that lasted forever, he replied, "Yes. I have kept it with me always, and I am looking at that same Etch-A- Sketch right now."

My son is alive! I have a son! I am speaking to my child! The thoughts are rushing through my head as fast as the emotions are running through my heart. He is not standing in front of me for me to look him in the eyes and know who he is, but it is worth the chance. My defenses are down, and I will make him prove me wrong. We finish up our conversation and promise to talk the next day when we have more time and can soak this in a little more. Over the next few days, we talk often and find out that we have much in common. I also find out more of the story that kept us apart. I know my side of it and proceed to find out about him.

Years after his supposed death, Ross was making his way through life and was dealing with some hard issues in his life. I know what it feels like to grow up with a stand-in dad, and it makes me sad to think that Ross didn't have his real dad there to help him with these times in his life. It is all too familiar to me. Ross had been told that I had abandoned him and that he had been adopted by his stepdad. He grew up using his stepdad's last name. Until one day he applied for credit and was turned down. The reason given was that the name on his application did not match his social security number. He is already not having an easy time, and this is one more thing that is frustrating his efforts in life. They won't tell him what his other name is and are suspicious that he is trying to steal someone else's identity. What now? Can't he catch a break? How does he figure this one out?

Ross makes a call to his sister and is venting about the list of all the things that are going wrong in his life. His sister finally tells him that according to her dad, Ross's dad was always a good man and did not deserve everything that happened to him. Maybe it is time to get in touch with his real dad, and maybe his real dad could be of help, even if it is only advice and moral support. Ross replies with frustration. Why should he make the effort to contact a man that has made no attempt to establish contact for the last ten years? His sister tells Ross that she may know why that happened. She tells Ross the story of what her dad, my old best friend, found out before his mother-in-law passed away. She told him the story of how she and her daughter didn't want Ross to go find his dad and how they came up with the story of falsifying his death to me. To add insult to great injury, Ross finds out that his stepdad never adopted him, and his last name is still Smith.

Talk about pulling the rug out from under a young man's world. He finds out that the truth was lies and that even more lies were told to cover up the truth. This is all too familiar to me, but I hate that this is happening to my own son. I know how much this hurts, and I don't want him to experience the same things that I have known. He and I spend a lot of time catching up. Catching up on happiness, regret, loss, and love. Kinda sounds like a country song. In a short amount of time, all of the pain that this has brought to my life begins to be swallowed up by the restoration of my son. Like the sun burning away the darkness of a foggy morning, my life, which is good, is made even brighter. In the Bible, God says that he will restore the years that the locusts have taken. That the years of toil and trials will not be in vain. I am not calling my ex-wife a locust. I am thankful to God for bringing my son back. An added bonus is that for the first time, I am feeling like a dad again. I have a son. I now have a legacy of my own to pass on to the next generation. I have a son who is watching to see what kind of man his own father is. What will I show him about living, loving, working, using your talents, embracing your destiny, and what it is to be a man? This is the biggest answer to the question of why I am doing this now.

One more coincidence in my life. I was twenty-seven when I found my birth mom. Ross was twenty-seven when he found me. We both made the effort, and we both are experiencing life with a parent that we lived without for too many years.

After reconnecting with Ross, he flew out to see me. Our last conversation was right before he got on the plane. I could tell that he was hesitant about something. He finally told me what was bothering him. He was embarrassed for me to know that he had tattoos, and he did not want me to think badly about him. I laughed. It's okay. I have scars. Tattoos are just scars that you choose. They tell a story about your life. Just like scars do. Hey. That rhymes too.

What Now?

As I am writing this, we are in the middle of negotiating for a publishing contract and a new music deal. We never imagined that it would be this difficult. It has been quite a journey. I at times have a simplistic view of life, and I pictured it being much easier. Kind of like "Hi. Elvis is my daddy, and I can sing." I imagined that this would be followed with generous offers to sing and become famous. Why wouldn't it? It seems obvious to me. It has not happened this way. Instead, it has turned into a long process. One of those journeys in life when you don't see the reasons for things that are happening until much later. We have learned, and are still learning, that things happen for a reason. The things that we call roadblocks God calls protecting us. We have had several people come and go during this process. We have learned a lot about learning to wait, patience, and perseverance. We have also learned that the time of waiting will show the character of those that you are waiting with. I have found myself surrounded with many people that support the idea of what I am doing and have made commitments to join me in this endeavor. These same people get scarce quickly when it is time to put their money where their mouth is. These days I have been struggling to make it.

Playing gigs locally doesn't pay what it used to. Actually, that is not quite true. It pays exactly what it used to. In an evening, I now make what I used to make when I was fourteen years old singing at the pizza joint. There are so many artists that want to perform now that restaurants and clubs don't have to pay much to get people to come and play. Most performers have full-time jobs and are doing this as a hobby. This makes it more difficult to make a living at this level. Everyone is full of ideas of what I should do, especially when they have a drink in their hand, but they disappear when it is time to put the plan into motion. Funny thing is none of them is concerned about how they are going to make it through the winter. They are all doing just fine. And apparently, I would be too if I just took their advice.

There have also been several people that have made serious offers to me. These offers have been to give me a recording or a management contract or some other offer to promote me to the top. I have found out a few things. One of them is that I do not need to be at the top. I am fine with being me, however far that takes me. Another thing that I have finally learned is that money, or the thought of money, changes most people. These offers to take me straight to the top would have left me with the crumbs of my success while they would be feasting on the rewards of my efforts. One person even generously offered to let me keep 15 percent of all that I made while he kept the rest of it. All because he would introduce me to the right people. Sadly, this is not abnormal for an artist that is desperate to get a record deal. Any record deal. Even iTunes is in on it. I have nothing against iTunes. They have revolutionized how music is purchased. They changed everything for the consumer while everything stays the same for the artist. iTunes has nothing to do with this. It is the contract that artists are wrapped up in with the record label. For every 99¢ song that sells, iTunes keeps one-third, and the rest goes to the label and the artist. Out of the 99¢, the artist averages 8–14¢ of each song purchased. I now realize something about me. At this stage of my life, I am no longer desperate for a deal. I am also not a show pony that will be trotted out on the whim of a record executive to show me off over and over again. This is why this road that we have chosen has taken us a little more than three years to get to this point. It has not been easy, and we have had to do a lot by ourselves. During this time, we have still been used and taken advantage of, but at least we know that it may happen, and we are more in control of what happens than I have ever been in my life. Being worn out at times has never felt so good.

I don't want this to come across the wrong way. I am not complaining. I know that this is my dream. I can't expect other people to feel the same way about my life that I do. This dream that I have has been a long time coming. It has taken several different directions and has changed many times along the way. I have to confess that I have played a major role in the delay of my dream. It is only coming to me now, later in life, for several reasons. The primary reason is that I still don't know what I want to do when I grow up. I don't have only one thing that I am focused on. I have been successful in several areas of life. I have performed for large crowds, written hit songs, been a cowboy, won rodeo competitions, had business ideas, started and developed businesses, made and lost a lot of money in multilevel marketing, started foundations, worked with charities, developed a school curriculum, had my own security business, worked as a sheriff's deputy and a bounty hunter. On and on it goes. For a large part of my life, I have not been focused on my singing career, but I always return to it. Singing has been the source of my greatest triumphs, and I have also experienced some of my lowest moments. I remember standing in the shower before a concert and, in that private moment, breaking down in tears. I was in a band that had a manager that was never pleased. I knew that I was preparing to go out onstage and would give it my all. I would give away all that I had to the audience. I also knew that when I walked offstage, standing there would be a man that could not do what I do, but he would have a head full of ideas of what I did wrong and what I should do differently. Not being able to please him no matter what I did was frustrating and disheartening to me. It took the joy away that I normally receive back from the crowd. This was probably the lowest I ever felt about performing.

No matter how many times I head off in a different direction, music always calls me back. It is a God-given gift that I can not outrun. I sang at a funeral service last year and then sang at the reception afterward. During the course of the evening, a woman came up to me and spoke to me. It caught me off guard and showed me again the power of music to reach the soul. It was an enjoyable reception as the man that had died lived a long and full life. It was a lively crowd, and I was singing some hymns as well as some popular older songs such as Sinatra. This lady approached me and, with a sense of urgency, grabbed my arm with one hand and my hand with the other. She locked eyes with me and told me that she didn't know who I was, but that when I sing, she feels the hand of God on her. She wanted to know who I was and how I did that to her. This caught me completely off guard. How do you answer a question like this? As much as it pains me, I have to admit that at times, I take what I do for granted. I have lived with it all my life, and I don't always remember how the music really does touch the deepest parts of the human soul. I need to be reminded sometimes. This was one more time of God reaching out and telling me that he gave me this gift for a reason. I am to use it to make a difference in this world. My mom tells me that I can run all I want to, but I can't ever outrun God.

Age and a little bit more maturity do bring clarity. I am seeing now that I have an opportunity with what I have been given and a responsibility for what I have received. I do not plan to reach the whole world. My desire is to do what I can and what I enjoy and see how far it goes. I no longer want to be the next Elvis. I want to be the only John Smith. I know that can't happen. Just look in the phone book. There are thousands of us. But you know what I mean. Sometimes we are only meant to really touch one or two lives, and that is the starting point for those few to go reach more. Only time will tell. I do know this. After all the years, all the miles, the joy, the heartbreak, the questions, and the answers, I am on the right road, with the best people around me, and I am looking forward to the journey as never before.

I have lived with comparisons to Elvis Presley all of my life. I have not gone looking for it. It comes to me. It has become commonplace that when I sing, someone compares my voice to Elvis. This even happens when I am singing my own songs. It happens so often that a couple of years ago, I started to tell a little bit of my story and where I come from. I fully expected to be met with laughter and disbelief at the outrageous events that are my life. I and those close to me have been surprised by the responses. The overwhelming reaction has been that it makes sense and explains a lot. It then leads to a whole lot of questions. I reply that one day the story may come out. They ask me to let them know because they can't wait to hear about it. It brings back some of their best memories of their youth. A favorite song can take you back to another place and time. They have just been taken back there by a combination of my voice and the story of Elvis. They get to relive these times in their lives, and it is rewarding to be a part of their enjoyment.

I don't know where this road is leading me, but I do know that it is going to be quite a ride. Thank you for picking up this book and listening to my life. I can't express to you how grateful I am that you are now a part of it. As Lawrence Welk was so excited to have found me when he was seventy-five years old, I am now fifty-one, and I feel like after all the life I have lived that I am just getting started. This is the end of the book, and the story is just beginning.

God bless you, and get ready. Here we come. I look forward to meeting each and every one of you.

Thank you. Thank you very much.

Signed: Elvis and Sherrill, Happy Birthday to Johnny

Sherrill, HT, and Marie

Elvis, Priscilla, my mom, and Glen Campbell

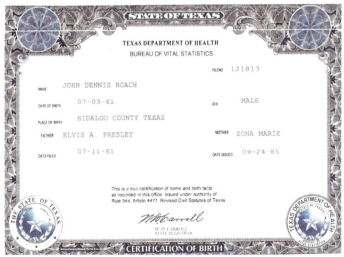

My birth certificate listing Elvis as my father

Elvis, December 1940

Johnny and Elvis

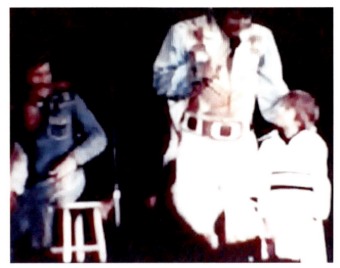

Sherrill, Elvis, and Johnny

Etta and Ruth McMasters with Lawrence

Johnny on a bus

Johnny on Elvis's tour bus

Zona Marie and daughter Susan

Little Johnny in his Sunday best

Johnny's version of Hee Haw

John the ring bearer

John on stage in Shreveport

Action Line article about John

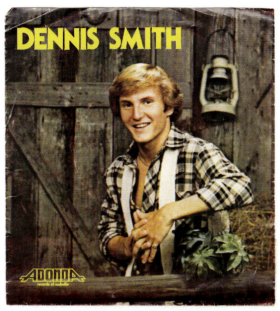

45 covers, front and back

records of nashville

PRESENTS

DENNIS SMITH

"I think Dennis is the best singer I've found in my lifetime. As you can see, even at my age of 75 I've found this good singer and I'm in Heaven."

(Lawrence Welk, as reported in Shreveport Journal)

GET IT TOGETHER TOGETHER

"I've been very fortunate in having many of my songs recorded by some of the top stars—Elvis Presley, Dean Martin, Mickey Gilley, Frank Sinatra, Hank Williams, Jr., Eddy Arnold, to name just a few. But it was a double pleasure when Dennis Smith went into the studio for his first major recording session and recorded like he had been doing it all of his life. He did a super job on *Get It Together Together* and when you hear the cut you'll know that Dennis Smith is here to stay.

Baker Knight

CALIFORNIA CALLING

"I've written a lot of songs, some of which have been recorded by such artists as Ronnie McDowell, T. G. Shepperd, Christi Lane and Shaun Nielsen. But recently I attended Dennis Smith's recording session in Nashville and was thrilled at the depth of feeling in his singing—he certainly captured the style I had in mind when I co-wrote *California Calling*. Dennis has a real future—and that future is Music!!!"

Daniel Willis

Produced by	HARRISON TYNER and DON FOWLER	
Arranged by	HAROLD BRADLEY	
Engineered by	LES LADD	
Recorded at	WOODLAND SOUND STUDIOS	
	Nashville	
Backup Singers	JOE BABCOCK, SHAUN NIELSEN,	
	LOUIS NUNLEY, HERSHAL WIGINTON	

HARGUS "PIG" ROBBINS	Piano
HAROLD BRADLEY	Guitar
DALE SELLERS	Electric Guitar
RAY EDENTON	Rhythm Guitar
BUDDY HARMAN	Drums
HENRY STRZELECKI	Bass
HAL RUGG	Steel

38 MUSIC SQUARE EAST, SUITE 115, NASHVILLE, TENNESSEE 37203 (615) 244-4224

AMERICA'S COUNTRY RADIO HOT 150
OF ALL MAJOR & INDIE LABEL PRODUCT

SONG TITLE	ARTIST	SONG TITLE	ARTIST	SONG TITLE	ARTIST
JUKEBOX IN MY MIND	ALABAMA	YOU LIE	REBA McENTIRE	NOBODY CRIES IN TEXAS	RICK WILLIAMS
FALL A TEAR BECOMES A ROSE	K. WHITLEY W/ L. MORGAN	SHE'S MY ROCK AROUND THE	STORM SEYMOUR	FOOL THAT I AM	TY GREEN
FOURTEEN MINUTES OLD	DOUG STONE	WHEN SOMEBODY LOVES YOU	RESTLESS HEART	TELL ME I WAS DREAMING	D'ANNS
WANTED	ALAN JACKSON	I'M TOO USED TO LOVING YOU	JERRY JARAMILLO	IF YOU'RE NOT HERE BY CLOSING	PAM BAILY
DON'T GO OUT	TANYA TUCKER	LEAVIN'	JOEY DAVIS	MY HEART GOES RUNNING	VINCE MURPHY
MY PAST IS PRESENT	RODNEY CROWELL	I SURE HEARD HER SAY GOOD	EDDIE FRENCH	THE THINGS YOU LEFT BEHIND	MATRICA BERG
PRECIOUS THING	STEVE WARINER	WHO WERE YOU THINKING OF	TEXAS TORNADOS	YOU DONE ME WRONG	JEFF STEVENS/BULLETS
STORY OF LOVE	DESERT ROSE BAND	IN BETWEEN A ROCK AND A	HOLLY RONICK	WHERE DID WE GO RIGHT	LACY J DALTON
FELL IN LOVE	CARLENE CARTER	UNDER THE GUN	SUZY BOGGUSS	LIKE THE FLIP OF A COIN	WOODY WILLS
TOO COLD AT HOME	MARK CHESNUTT	HEART BEYOND REPAIR	WING TO WING	SITTIN UP WITH THE DEAD	RAY STEVENS
I MEANT EVERY WORD HE SAID	RICKY VAN SHELTON	LOVE KEEPS KNOCKING	SCOTT CARTER	LIVING FOR THE WEEKEND	DOYLE NELSON
BATTLE HYMN OF LOVE	K. MATTEA/T. O'BRIEN	WHAT IT DOLS TO ME	SWEETHEARTS OF RODEO	QUIETLY CRAZY	HAL GIBSON
I'M GONNA BE SOMEBODY	TRAVIS TRITT	GOOD AIN'T GOOD ENOUGH	DON ARTHUR	THE OTHER SIDE OF LOVE	GAIL DAVIES
PARADISE KNIFE AND GUN CLUB	JERRY LANSDOWNE	GREEN EYED ANGEL	JOAN BUCKLEY	WALKIN IN YOUR WOMAN'S SHOES	CORKI JO
THE ONE YOU'VE LEFT BEHIND	SYLVIA WINTERS	MISBEHAVIN SHOES	EDDIE BOND	TEN GALLON DREAMS	JOHN ANDREW PARIS
FOOL SUCH AS I	BAILEY & THE BOYS	IF THEY AIN'T GOT A FIDDLE	BENNY DEAN	COLD HARD LIGHT OF DAY	WANDA HANKINS
FRIENDS IN LOW PLACES	GARTH BROOKS	WORK SONG	CORBIN/HANNER	HARDTOP OF COUNTRY	JERRY LEE CHANCELER
BORN TO BE BLUE	THE JUDDS	YOU REALLY HAD ME GOING	HOLLY DUNN	EVERY BREATH YOU TAKE	WHITE LACE
MY HEART IS SET ON YOU	LIONEL CARTWRIGHT	TELL ME WHY	JOE BARNHILL	HUCKLEBERRY BOOGIE	R. B. STONE
DRINKING	GEORGE STRAIT	WESTERN GIRL	MARTY STUART	GUITAR TALK	JOHNATHAN EDWARDS
CHEATING LIST	DAWN ANITA	BETTER CLASS OF LOSERS	CHUCK GRISSON	I'M ON MY WAY TO TEXAS	CORI BREWSTER
I LOVE IT OUT TONIGHT	EDDIE SABBITT	100 YEARS TOO LATE	ROY FARRAR	STONEWASHED JEANS	LIZZIE ANN
SHE PUT THE MUSIC IN ME	CLINTON GREGORY	THERE'S A PHONE ON EVERY	SUSI BEATTY	YOU'RE STILL EVERY NOTE	LARRY WHALEY
LOST IN THE SHUFFLE	BENNY McARTHUR	WILL I LOVE AGAIN	JIM MARLBORO	EVERY TIME I THINK IT'S OVER	LES TAYLOR
I'LL LIE MYSELF TO SLEEP	SHELBY LYNNE	RIVER OF LOVE	KELLY WILLIS	SHADES	DEX HAVEN COUNTRY
YOUR LOVE	LINDA CAROL FORREST	WE NO TELL MOTEL	RITA EILEEN	LOOKING OUT FOR NUMBER 1	JOSIAH
I COULD BE PERSUADED	BELLAMY BROTHERS	HAPPY FOR YOUR SAKE	KIM TSOY	ACES	CHERYL WHEELER
RECKLESS HEART	SOUTHERN PACIFIC	WHEN I HAD YOU	KIMBERLY CARTER	THE OLD SOFT SHOE	KAREN JOHNS
WHEN IT RAINS IT POURS	MERLE HAGGARD	NOW 'BOUT US	GIRLS NEXT DOOR	CAN I COME BACK TO YOU	PERRY LAPOINTE
KEEPIN ME UP NIGHTS	ASLEEP AT THE WHEEL	PLAY ANOTHER GOOD OLD	CURTIS LEE CADY	TELL ME I'M WRONG	RICH GRISSOM
ALONG THE RIO GRANDE	BILL BEAVER	WALTZ ACROSS TEXAS	JENELL RAE	MY HEART KEEPS CHANGING	KENNETH SHEPHERD
LOVE IS STRANGE	K. ROGERS/D. PARTON	JUST CAN'T LET HIM GO	STEVE RHOADES	TEAR IT UP	JONI HARMS
SOMETHING OF A DREAMER	MARY C. CARPENTER	DANCE A LITTLE CLOSER	STOKER BROTHERS	HOT NIGHT IN A SMALL TOWN	BILLY AND AM SUNS
FEED THIS FIRE	ANNE MURRAY	HIT & RUN	THE CRUISERS	I'LL BE WAITING	LITTLE JOE
THIS AIN'T MY FIRST RODEO	VERN GOSDIN	MAN TO MAN	HANK WILLIAMS JR	ODE TO TOM LANDRY	TRAVIS LEWIS
DANCE IN CIRCLES	TIM RYAN	LOUISIANA NURSERY RHYME	BENNIE PRINCE	SHOWDOWN IN THE STREET	D. C. MARCUM
HONKY TONK BLUES	PIRATES OF THE MISS	PERFECT COMBINATION	DANNY ROY	HIGH SCHOOL DAYS	VERN BRENNN
LET ME BE THE ONE	TOUCH OF COUNTRY	FEEL LIKE I'M FALLING	HOLLY LIPTON	MAMMA DIDN'T RAISE NO FOOL	DAWN DOMINIC
PLEASE LET ME LOVE YOU	JON DENNIS SMITH	NEVER ENDING SONG OF LOVE	CRYSTAL GAYLE	I'LL ALWAYS REMEMBER YOU	MONA LISA
LET'S CALL IT A DAY TODAY	TAMMY WYNETT	EMPTY SEAT BESIDE ME	CHRIS WALL	WORKIN YOUR WAY TO MY HEART	KEVIN CRONNIN
NOTHING CAN STOP MY	DAVIES/KATH HOUSTON	YOU CAN HOLD HER	MARY DANNA	GIVIN UP EASY	KEVIN FRANCI
BOOGIE AND BEETHOVEN	GATLIN BROTHERS	THINKING BOUT YOU	SUSAN ROSIE MANNING	LONG NECKIN AND LOVIN	CHE FLANE
FOOL OF A HEART	LIVE & KICKIN	YOU BEAT ALL I'VE EVER SEEN	LISA RICH	DADDY'S FADED PICTURES	DIANNA GILLASPY
DANGEROUSLY LONELY	JOHNNY LEE	FOOLISH PRIDE	MARCY CARR	TONIGHT YOUR PILLOW ROSE IS	AUDREY NUNNELET
EARLY AMERICAN ROCK	GARY RAY	JUST AS LONG AS YOU'LL BE	VALARIE WILSON	HONKY TONK ROSE	KIMBALL WIN
HE WAS ON TO SOMETHING	RICKY SKAGGS	YOU MADE LIFE GOOD AGAIN	NITTY GRITTY DIRT BND	HANGIN OUT	CARLENE
NOTHING'S GONNA BOTHER ME	FORESTER SISTERS	HERE COMES ANOTHER LONELY	ALLEN KARL	STILL LIFE	CHARLES GOODMAN
SOUTHERN FRAME OF MIND	HEATH LOCKLEAR	CRAZY IN LOVE	CONWAY TWITTY	ALL THE MAGIC'S GONE	JIMMY SNYDER
HOME	JOE DIFFIE	HE MADE A WOMAN OUT OF ME	JANET DAVID	DON'T WORRY ABOUT ME	RUSTY GILLAM
ALABAMA CLAY	JOEY RELLO				

John at #39 for radio Hot 150

Send to printer   Close window

Lawrence Welk

The Champagne Music Man bubbles on, and on, and on...

BY HELEN ZUKOWSKI

Lawrence Welk, the Champagne Music King

FROM THE PALM SPRINGS LIFE ARCHIVE

Reprinted from the January 1979 issue of Palm Springs Life *magazine*

It's 10:30 Tuesday morning in Studio 31 at CBS, and they're well into rehearsal for the umpteen-hundreth taping of the Most Unlikely Success Story on Television.

In a medium where slickness is next to godliness, where songs turn over faster than Disneyland turnstiles, and where disposability has become a way of life, "The Lawrence Welk Show," now in its 23rd television season, has to be the anomaly of anomalies.

To begin with, look at the star, the musical don, Numero Uno, Lawrence Welk. By any showbiz standards, this very nice seventy-five-year-old man who believes in the family, God's Laws, the old-time values, who abhors sex and violence on the screen, and who (by his own admission) doesn't "know how" to smoke or drink, wouldn't exactly prompt a starmaker to drool with anticipation.

Article about Lawrence Welk that mentions John

When ABC first launched the Lawrence Welk Show in 1955, howls of disbelief rose from the critics and one noted orchestra leader snorted, "He stumbles all over the stage and his band plays corny arrangements that we threw away 15 years ago. Who is this SQUARE?"

Twenty-three years later, the "square" is number one in the hearts of millions and the hotshot bandleader has long since been discarded on some musical ash heap. In fact, at the networks Lawrence once earned the moniker "The Meatgrinder" because of the way he eliminated competitors who were thrown into timeslots against the show. The casualties — Jimmy Durante, Herb Shriner, Janis Paige, Robert Montgomery and Sid Caesar, to name a few — form a veritable "Who's Who" of showbiz.

One almost biblical rule of thumb with the variety folks is to hire big name stars as feature guests. On the Lawrence Welk Show, there are no guest stars, only the regulars, the Lawrence Welk "family."

"For me," Welk says, "there is no greater joy than taking someone everybody says doesn't stand a chance and making a winner out of him. We don't hire stars. We create them."

Relentless critics say he simply rolls out Barbie Doll androids that look and sound alike — cookie cutter Lennon Sisters in an endless procession of Welk-en-kinder. But in the cold, cruel and competitive entertainment world, he stands almost alone as a person who bolsters, supports, finances, coaches, encourages and, generally, lends an avuncular ear to hopeful young talent.

Throughout his career, he's almost made an industry of giving "the big break" to any talented young person who shows he or she knows what he wants and is willing to work (hard!) for it.

The Welk training program consists of an intense one-year trial period during which the young talent works with regular members of the show and puts in occasional guest appearances. There are no signed contracts, no promises, no guarantees — but if, at the end of the year, the young performer shows he has learned enough self-discipline, has developed musically, and has the drive to score favorably when assessed on some metaphorical Welk Performance Chart, he'll be absorbed into the show when there's an opening. Two of the newest aspirants are Teresa Dorman and Dennis Smith.

On this particular Tuesday, Teresa, 22, a blonde knockout in black chiffon, has come up from Escondido and sits beside Uncle Lawrence in the dressing room. Even though she's heard it many times before, she listens in rapt attention, her eyes never leaving his face, while Lawrence explains how Teresa had a problem with her pronunciation.

Her therapy was to play, over and over again, Rosemary Clooney records that Lawrence sent down to Escondido. Teresa, while training, lives in the Escondido mobile home community owned by the Welk corporation and works as a singing hostess in the community's restaurant.

Would I like to hear Teresa sing? Lawrence sets the tempo with a little baton and she happily warbles a few lines of a song. Lawrence beams his approval.

Dennis Smith joins the group. Dennis, 17, connected with the show when it was visiting his home town in Louisiana. He'd taken two elderly aunts to see Lawrence and at the end of the evening, when the audience was invited up on stage to dance, Dennis asked if he could sing instead, since he didn't dance too well. After he had finished his number, someone shouted, "Why don't you hire him?" and Lawrence replied, "We will."

Would I also like to hear Dennis sing? Dennis smiles an aw-shucks grin and sets into "Love Me Tender" a cappella. Lawrence again turns, beams his approval, and suggests Dennis try it once again, "but clean it up a little."

Without a pause, Dennis tears into a cleaner version of the song. Good, good, but Lawrence suggests it one more time, half a tone higher. Without a flicker of protest, his grin suitably fastened, Dennis is again out-Presleying Presley.

Others drift in and out, paying obeisance, asking advice, joking, and you begin to sense what it is about the Musical Family that has made it so appealing to so many people for so many years. To begin with, there's a magnetic solidarity

article about Lawrence Welk (cont'd)

The Lawrence Welk years

Ad and ticket to The Lawrence Welk Show

Lawrence Welk

Welk bubbling over singer

Lawrence Welk was bubbling with excitement during a telephone interview from his Santa Monica, Calif., headquarters.

"I hit the jackpot this morning," the 75-year-old orchestra leader and television star said.

Welk said he had just talked to a young country singer he had discovered on a recent tour. The boy, although too young now, wanted to join Welk's orchestra when he was older.

"I think he's the best singer I've ever found in my lifetime," he said. "As you can see, even now at my age of 75, I've found this good singer and I'm in heaven this morning.

Welk said that his formula for success is the same thing he would tell aspiring young musicians: "Learn how to please people...so that they will enjoy themselves."

Today the Lawrence Welk Network numbers more than 250 stations in the U.S. and Canada, and is watched weekly by an audience estimated at more than 36 million people.

_____ that holds

"I hit the jackpot this morning," the 75-year-old orchestra leader and television star said.

Welk said he had just talked to a young country singer he had discovered on a recent tour. The boy, although too young now, wanted to join Welk's orchestra when he was older.

"I think he's the best singer I've ever found in my lifetime," he said. "As you can see, even now at my age of 75, I've found this good singer and I'm in heaven this morning.

Welk said that his formula for success is the same thing he would tell aspiring young musicians: "Learn how to please people...so that they will enjoy themselves."

Today the Lawrence Welk Network numbers more than 250 stations in the U.S. and Canada, and is watched weekly by an audience estimated at more than 36 million people.

The force that holds Welk's "musical family" together is, he said, God's law.

"The reason I mention God's law is because, as you can see, the minute you create a condition which is a sin, it pulls people down a notch. Once the sin has embedded in them...the people are not strong enough to get rid of it anymore. So, by the folks knowing we operate this way, they become part of it. We have much less trouble.

An article from Shreveport about Lawrence Welk

ID and Deep South Quartet

John's first 45: Green, Green Grass of Home

PROCLAMATION

WHEREAS, many years ago, before ELVIS PRESLEY, the "King of Rock & Roll", was married to his wife Priscilla, he had dated a number of women, both famous and some not-so-famous, and

WHEREAS, a young lady from Shreveport, Louisiana, by the name of Zona Marie Anderson Roach, met Elvis and became romantically involved with him for a period of time, and

WHEREAS, according to Ms. Roach, she became pregnant with the child of Elvis, but due to various circumstances at the time, including the fact that she was a divorced woman and Elvis was a rising star she and Elvis were unable to get married, and

WHEREAS, a decision was made by Elvis and Marie to give the baby up for adoption, and

WHEREAS, that baby was raised as JOHN D. SMITH, and became an accomplished musician, and only learned of his true parentage much later in life when he was finally able to track down his birth mother who advised him of the identity of his biological father, and

WHEREAS, JOHN D. SMITH, who now is known as "JOHN D. SMITH PRESLEY", has now decided that, for the first time to publicly announce his claimed paternity and to do so in the Council Chambers of the Municipal Council of the City of Egg Harbor, and

IN APPRECIATION of JOHN D. SMITH PRESLEY coming to the City of Egg Harbor to make this announcement, and in further consideration of the fact that he may very well be the son of ELVIS AARON PRESLEY, the greatest and most famous Rock and Roll Performer in our history.

I, JOSEPH A. KUEHNER, JR., Mayor of the City of Egg Harbor declare today, Thursday, the 14th of April, JOHN D. SMITH PRESLEY DAY.

Joseph A. Kuehner Jr., Mayor
April 14, 2011

John Smith Presley proclamation

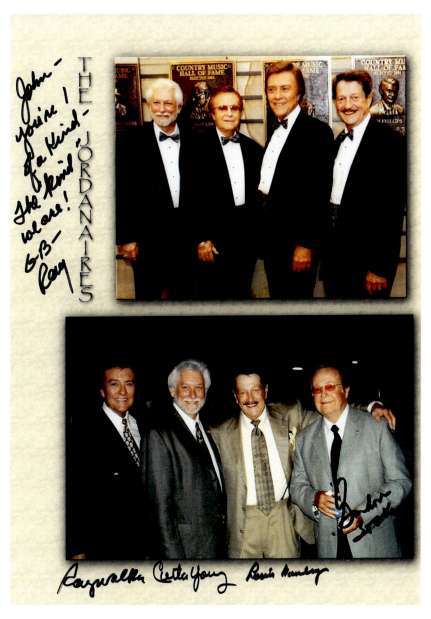

Jordanaires

Excelsior Music press photo

The Rich Clarity of
Jon Dennis Smith
& Southern Thunder

EXCELSIOR MUSIC MANAGEMENT
For further information and bookings, call 1-800-727-5828
In Texas call (214) 586-7528, or (214) 580-7630

first
american
RECORDS, INC.
NASHVILLE

Southern Thunder

Envelope that goes with the letter from HT

Cabaret Bar in Bandera, Texas

DJ RADIO SINDAL   MAILING ADDRESS
WRITER TRAIL MAGAZINE   BJARNE CHRISTENSEN
MEMBER OF S C C   UGILTVEJ 900
RADIO PLAYLIST   LOERSLEV
    9800 HJOERRING
DATE: _FEBR. 20 1992_   DENMARK
LIVE/PHONE INTERVIEW: PHONE + 45 98 96 31 05

NO	TITLE	ARTIST	COMPANY
1	COUNTRY IN GOOD OLD GERMANY	NASHVILLE MUSIC COMPANY	RANGER REC
2	TAKE IT EASY NIMMS LEICHT	TOM ASTOR	AMC REC
3	LOUISIANA SATURDAY NIGHT	JOHN BRACK	ARIOLA REC
4	DADDY IS THE BEST	SPITCASTLE BULLWASHERS	DIE MÜHLE REC
5	WAITING FOR A SECOND WIND	MOONLIGHT RIDERS	MARLSTONE REC
6	BLUE WING	ERIC ROBINSON	MSA REC
7	LOVE'S JUST A SLOW SONG AWAY	LEE ANN ALLISON	TENN. STAR. TRAKS
8	I DON'T WANT TO HURT	ALMA	TN. STAR TRAKS
9	ONLY A COWBOY UNDERSTANDS	MOMENTUM BAND	ROYALTY REC
10	AS IF I DIDN'T KNOW	DESIREE	ROYALTY REC
11	TEXAS ON MY MIND	GREG PAUL	ROYALTY REC
12	SLIPPIN' AWAY	TINETA	ROYALTY REC
13	IF TEARDROPS WERE PENNIS	MYRNA LORRIE	TN. STAR TRAKS
14	SURE CURE FOR THE BLUES	JON DENNIS SMITH	TN. STAR TRAKS
15	LOOKING BACK	CATHY DALE	TN. STAR TRAKS
16	ALL I NEED IS YOU	LYNNE & THE REBELS	TN STAR TRAKS
17	THAT WAS BEFORE I MET YOU	DOUG JUDSON	TN. STAR TRAKS
18	MOIN (WRONG)	TOM ASTOR	AMC REC
19	RASTLOSE MÄNNER	NASHVILLE MUSIC COMPANY	RANGER REC
20			

Danish Country DJ song chart

Happy Hill Farms program

Susan, Zona Marie, and John. Mother's Day, 2000.

BROUGHT TO YOU BY
RICH N FAMOUS GUITARS

RICH CARLBURG

Rich N Famous Custom Guitars

RICH@RICHNFAMOUSGUITARS.COM

RICHNFAMOUSGUITARS.COM